Psychology of Emotions, Motivations and Actions

nova
Medicine & Health

Psychology of Emotions, Motivations and Actions

Understanding Emotions
Michael A. Carr (Editor)
2021. ISBN: 978-1-68507-307-7 (Softcover)
2021. ISBN: 978-1-68507-325-1 (eBook)

Bring My Smile Back: Working with Unhappy Children in Education
Maria A. Efstratopoulou (Editor)
2020. ISBN: 978-1-53617-277-5 (Hardcover)
2020. ISBN: 978-1-53617-278-2 (eBook)

How Culture Shapes Suicidal Behavior
David Lester, Ph.D. (Editor)
2019. ISBN: 978-1-53615-098-8 (Softcover)
2019. ISBN: 978-1-53615-099-5 (eBook)

Post-Traumatic Stress Disorder: New Research
Edward Foreman and Jay Fuller (Editors)
2013. ISBN: 978-1-62417-437-7 (Hardcover)
2013. ISBN: 978-1-62417-438-4 (eBook)

Psychotic Depression in the Elderly
Rajesh R. Tampi, MD (Editor)
2011. ISBN: 978-1-62100-330-4 (Online Book)

More information about this series can be found at
https://novapublishers.com/product-category/series/psychology-of-emotions-motivations-and-actions/

James J. Carmona
Editor

The Importance of Self-Efficacy and Self-Compassion

nova
Medicine & Health

NOTICE TO THE READER

Library of Congress Cataloging-in-Publication Data

ISBN: 978-1-68507-763-1

Published by Nova Science Publishers, Inc. † New York

Contents

Preface

Self-efficacy and self-compassion are psychological skills that form the basis for resilience, success, and overall quality of life, and as such understanding how best to implement these skills is essential for well-being. This volume includes six chapters that explore the concepts of self-efficacy and self-compassion from several perspectives. Chapter One investigates the predictive value of pre-academic self-efficacy for academic self-efficacy six months into the Danish teacher education program. Chapter Two provides a theoretical foundation for educator self-efficacy and current empirical evidence exploring self-efficacy of educators who are working in schools implementing tiered systems. Chapter Three examines reciprocal relations between academic self-efficacy and elements of achievement in math, with persistence as a mediator. Chapter Four synthesizes and examines research evidence on the relationship between parental self-compassion and parents' mental health, analyzes the role of parental self-compassion in parenting practices, and investigates the effects of parents' self-compassion on children's outcomes. Chapter Five reviews recent findings concerning self-compassion from a trait/state perspective based on a development schema theory combined with a state of mind approach. Lastly, Chapter Six explores self-efficacy and its association with demographic characteristics in Greek families of university students with or without members with special educational needs and disabilities during the COVID-19 pandemic.

Chapter 1 - Academic self-efficacy is a central concept for higher education. Much research has been conducted on the predictive value of academic self-efficacy in relation to educational outcomes and many studies have compared the academic self-efficacy of diverse subgroups of students, while few of these studies have investigated academic self-efficacy measures for invariance. The role of pre-academic self-efficacy for educational outcomes or as a predicter of later academic self-efficacy is an area with little research. The current study was aimed at investigating the predictive value of pre-academic self-efficacy for academic self-efficacy six months into the Danish teacher education program, and as the first study in the field using targeted measures for the two self-efficacy constructs. The psychometric properties of the measures, including invariance, were investigated using item response theory models prior to the main analysis. Participants were 407 Danish students admitted to the teacher education program, who completed the pre-academic learning self-efficacy scale after they knew they had been admitted but prior to commencing the program, as well as the current academic learning self-efficacy scale after six months. The prediction analysis was conducted using general linear models with the inclusion of background information as additional independent variables. The results showed that both pre-academic learning self-efficacy and age at the time of admission predicted current academic learning self-efficacy six months later, with pre-academic learning self-efficacy contributing the most and positively to current academic learning self-efficacy and age contributing very little and negatively to the prediction. The study points to a new direction in academic self-efficacy research, namely to uncover how self-efficacy changes and evolves throughout various higher education degree programs using targeted measures, and how longitudinally determined patterns – rather than time-point measures – of academic self-efficacy might be associated with educational outcomes.

Chapter 2 - Educator wellbeing is promoted when school leaders communicate a clear and sustained vision and provide adequate resources and professional learning opportunities to achieve positive outcomes for students. In this chapter, the authors provide a theoretical foundation for educator self-efficacy and current empirical evidence exploring self-efficacy of educators who are working in schools implementing tiered systems. The authors begin with an overview of the theoretical and empirical literature on the importance of educator self-efficacy and wellbeing when engaging in systems efforts. Then, the authors provide a brief overview of tiered systems. Next, the authors provide a summary of research conducted to date that examined how teachers fare when working in tiered systems. Then, the authors discuss core features of tiered systems that promote educators' wellbeing and minimize burnout. The authors conclude with considerations for educators engaging in system change to promote students' educational outcomes.

Chapter 3 - Social cognitive learning theory postulates indirect relations between academic self-efficacy and achievement mediated via persistence. Furthermore, it anticipates reciprocal relations between academic self-efficacy and achievement, but only if scholastic achievement is reported back to the students' and perceived as individual success. The present study examines reciprocal relations between academic self-efficacy and elements of achievement (grades and test results) in math, with persistence as a mediator. It also examines gender differences and differences between students from immigrant and non-immigrant backgrounds. Data collected from 1,597 students at the beginning of 7th grade and 1,312 at the end were analyzed with bootstrap testing and multigroup structural equation models. Results emphasized the importance of academic self-efficacy for math achievement mediated via persistence. Subgroup-specific results indicate that gender stereotypes and socio-cultural values shape academic self-perceptions.

Chapter 4 - In this chapter, firstly, the authors synthesize and examine research evidence on the relationship between parental self-compassion and parents' mental health. Secondly, the authors look into the role of parental self-compassion in parenting practices, such as reducing harmful parenting approaches while promoting positive parenting practices to strengthen the parent-child relationship. Thirdly, the authors investigate the direct and indirect effect of parents' self-compassion on children's outcomes (e.g., reducing problem behaviors and increasing quality of life). To conclude this chapter, the authors propose some suggestions for future research and practice to apply self-compassion to improve the quality of parenting.

Chapter 5 - Self-compassion has been described as an adaptive psychological domain that allows individuals to be kind to themselves and to others when confronted with personal flaws and inadequacies. In the face of a situation of suffering caused by oneself or/and others, self-compassion facilitates feelings of warmth, caring and affection, which signal an emotional need to overcome emotional distress. Previous research has associated self-compassion with psychological well-being, life satisfaction and psychological flexibility, and the regulation of psychological needs, suggesting that self-compassion can be seen as an adaptive self-domain. In addition, self-compassion measured as a psychological trait was associated with mindfulness and self-acceptance traits, and measured as a state of mind, was associated with early maladaptive schemas. In this sense, self-compassion can function as both: a psychological trait and a state. However, this distinction does not seem clear. Therefore, this chapter aims to contribute to that clarification by reviewing recent findings from a trait/state perspective based on a development schema theory combined with a state of mind approach. Suggestions for future research are also outlined to clarify whether self-compassion might be better conceptualized as a trait and/or as psychological state.

Chapter 6 - *Background*: The COVID-19 pandemic engendered a new reality and considerable changes, with multiple psychological consequences for individuals and families. The COVID-19 pandemic and its subsequent containment are unprecedented global stressors. Research suggests that self-efficacy is one of the key resources for managing stressful events and reducing the associated risks. Self-efficacy is a general concept referring to the extent to which people believe they have the competency to cope adequately with stressful life demands or challenges.

Objectives: This study aims to explore self-efficacy and its association with demographic characteristics in Greek families of university students with or without members with special educational needs and disabilities (SEND) during the COVID-19 pandemic in Greece.

Methods: The study population consisted of 411 participants, 130 men και 281 women, of which the 194 were children (university students) in the 3rd and 4th years of their studies and the 217 were parents. The age of participants ranged from 20 to 60 years. A self-report questionnaire and the Self-efficacy Scale (GSE) were used for data collection.

Results: According to the findings, participants (total sample) showed a high degree of self-efficacy during the COVID-19 pandemic and specific demographic characteristics seemed to have a significant association with self-efficacy. On one hand, there were associations between self-efficacy and a) sex, b) the family type, and d) the employment status. In particular, a higher degree of self-efficacy was shown in males, the nuclear and the extended families, the participants with no employment, and the individuals who worked from home. On the other hand, self-efficacy was not statistically significant concerning the family role (parent or child), the level of education, the existence or non-existence of one or more members with SEND in the family, and the marital status.

Conclusion: The study's main conclusion was that university students' families with or without members with SEND activated self-efficacy as a mechanism for preserving their balance during the COVID-19 pandemic and that specific individual and family demographic characteristics affect the degree of self-efficacy.

Chapter 1

Predicting Student Teachers' Academic Learning Self-Efficacy at the Second Semester from Their Pre-Academic Learning Self-Efficacy

Tine Nielsen[*], **PhD**
Associate Professor, UCL University College
[UCL Erhvervsakademi og Professionshoejskole], Odense, Denmark

Abstract

Academic self-efficacy is a central concept for higher education. Much research has been conducted on the predictive value of academic self-efficacy in relation to educational outcomes and many studies have compared the academic self-efficacy of diverse subgroups of students, while few of these studies have investigated academic self-efficacy measures for invariance. The role of pre-academic self-efficacy for educational outcomes or as a predicter of later academic self-efficacy is an area with little research. The current study was aimed at investigating the predictive value of pre-academic self-efficacy for academic self-efficacy six months into the Danish teacher education program, and as the first study in the field using targeted measures for the two self-efficacy constructs. The psychometric properties of the measures, including invariance, were investigated using item response theory models prior to the main analysis. Participants were 407 Danish students admitted to the teacher education program, who completed the pre-academic learning self-efficacy scale after they knew they had been admitted but prior to commencing the program, as well as the current

[*] Corresponding Author's Email: tini@ucl.dk.

In: The Importance of Self-Efficacy and Self-Compassion
Editor: James J. Carmona
ISBN: 978-1-68507-763-1

academic learning self-efficacy scale after six months. The prediction analysis was conducted using general linear models with the inclusion of background information as additional independent variables. The results showed that both pre-academic learning self-efficacy and age at the time of admission predicted current academic learning self-efficacy six months later, with pre-academic learning self-efficacy contributing the most and positively to current academic learning self-efficacy and age contributing very little and negatively to the prediction. The study points to a new direction in academic self-efficacy research, namely to uncover how self-efficacy changes and evolves throughout various higher education degree programs using targeted measures, and how longitudinally determined patterns – rather than time-point measures – of academic self-efficacy might be associated with educational outcomes.

Keywords: pre-academic learning self-efficacy, current academic learning self-efficacy, prediction, Rasch model, graphical loglinear Rasch models

Introduction

Self-efficacy, at the general level, refers to the belief in one's own capability to plan and perform necessary actions to attain a certain outcome, while academic self-efficacy refers to such beliefs within the academic context or in relation to specific academic domains, disciplines, processes or tasks (Bandura, 1997). Students who feel efficacious when learning or performing a task have been found to work harder and persist longer when they encounter difficulties and achieve at a higher level of academic performance (Schunk & Pajares, 2002). An ongoing unresolved discussion in self-efficacy research is whether self-efficacy is a general or a specific construct, or something in between (Bandura, 1997; Pajares, 1997; Scherbaum, Cohen-Charash, & Kern, 2006). There exists a plethora of academic self-efficacy instruments, and they range from the altogether general, over the domain-specific, the context-specific, to the single-task-situated self-efficacy. The most common in educational research is to construe self-efficacy as at least domain-specific; e.g., the General Academic Self-Efficacy Scale (GASE; Nielsen, Dammeyer, Vang & Makransky, 2017), which is specific to the broader academic domain, or the Physics Self-Efficacy Questionnaire (PSEQ: Lindstrøm & Sharma, 2011), which is specific to the domain of physics education. At the other end of the spectrum are the task-situated self-efficacy measures used in studies of complex task-specific processes in a narrow context with no intent to compare this with other contexts; e.g., the task-specific self-efficacy scale developed by Yeo and Neal (2006) to judge confidence in achieving a range of possible performance levels on various air-traffic controller tasks. In between these are a range of sub-domain, context- and course-specific self-efficacy instruments; e.g., the commonly used specific academic self-efficacy scale from the Motivated Strategies of Learning Inventory (MSLQ; Pintrich, Smith, Garcia & McKeachie, 1991), which is course-specific and aimed at the context of higher secondary and tertiary education, as well as the adaptation of this scale into two "doubly-specific" scales, namely the Specific Academic Learning Self-Efficacy Scale and the Specific Academic Exam Self-Efficacy Scale (SAL-SE & SAE-SE), which are both course-specific and specific to either learning or taking exams (Nielsen, Makransky, Vang & Dammeyer, 2017). Self-efficacy is thus a central and much-used construct at many levels of specificity within the broad field of education.

Academic Self-Efficacy and Educational Outcomes

The positive correlational relationship between self-efficacy and academic performance is well-established (Ferla et al., 2009; Luszczynska et al., 2005; Zimmerman, Bandura & Martinez-Pons, 1992). Low self-efficacy has been found to be associated with increased risk of depression and anxiety (Luszczynska, et al., 2005; Muris, 2002; Tahmassian & Jalali Moghadam, 2011), and self-efficacy has been found to mitigate the negative effect of stress on life satisfaction (Burger & Samuel, 2017). Self-efficacy, self-esteem and psychological distress have been found to be the most important predictors of stress in university students (Saleh et al., 2017). Thus, self-efficacy plays a central though not direct role in relation to academic outcomes as it contributes to a general sense of well-being and mediates negative mental states.

Recent meta-analyses have concluded that self-efficacy is the strongest (non-ability) predictor of grade point average (GPA) in HE, being above personality traits, motivation and various learning strategies (Bartimote-Aufflick et al., 2015; Honicke & Broadbent, 2015; Richardson et al., 2012). Another recent meta-analysis suggests student self-efficacy to be heterogeneously associated with gender as the relationship is moderated by academic discipline (Huang, 2013). Given the importance of self-efficacy for educational outcomes, a large body of research has focused on investigating differences in levels of self-reported self-efficacy for student sub-groups, e.g., gender, age, and academic disciplines. While this is the case, only a few studies have determined whether the self-efficacy scales they used functioned in the same ways across such subgroups and thus delivered unbiased measures for their comparisons (Nielsen et al., 2017a).

The relationship between self-efficacy (measured after commencing higher education) and student persistence and attrition is also well studied. A meta-analysis concluded that student self-efficacy beliefs were associated with a variety of academic persistence outcomes such as number of terms completed, and number tasks completed (Multon, Brown & Lent, 1991). With regard to student attrition, both De Clercq, Galand and Frenay (2017) and Devonport and Lane (2006) found low academic self-efficacy in the first year at university was associated with an increased risk of dropping out. In addition, several studies have found a positive association between high academic self-efficacy and an increased completion intention at various time-points (Elliot, 2016; Lent et al., 2016; Thomas, 2014; Vuong, Brown-Welty & Tracz, 2010; Young, 2018). Again, none of these studies investigated the measurement invariance of the constructs used.

Pre-Academic Self-Efficacy and Educational Outcomes

The predictive power of academic self-efficacy prior to higher education for academic outcome has hardly been studied: Yong (2010) found no discipline-specific differences in general self-efficacy level in a study of 105 pre-university engineering and business students admitted to a private Malaysian university. Aryee (2017) found that high levels of pre-higher education mathematics self-efficacy were associated with student persistence and the completion of college, while low levels were associated with a lower likelihood of attaining any degree or credential. Van Herpen et al., (2017) found that general academic self-efficacy did not predict academic success in the first year in general (sample sizes were too small to investigate single disciplines), when assessed at the time of application to university. More recently, two Danish studies have studied what they term ‘Pre-Academic Learning Self-Efficacy’ (PAL-SE) and ‘Pre-Academic Exam Self-Efficacy’ (PAE-SE) as forms of academic self-efficacy concerned with the future higher education and measured just prior to commencement (Nielsen, Friderichsen & Hartkopf, 2019; Nielsen, 2021a). Nielsen and colleagues (2019) examined the psychometric properties of both the PAL-SE and the PAE-SE scale, and documented a need for adjusting the PAL-SE scores for item bias prior to comparison. In addition, they found that PAL-SE scores differed across students admitted to various university degree programs and that PAL-SE scores was associated with first-year attrition. Similarly for academic profession degree[1] students, Nielsen (2021a) also found it necessary to adjust PAL-SE scores for item bias and subsequently found that the adjusted PAL-SE scores differed across students admitted to various academy profession degree programs.

Changes in Academic Self-Efficacy during Higher Education

Changes in academic self-efficacy during the course of higher education have typically been studied in relation to specific courses or methods of teaching and have been focused on very specific forms of academic self-efficacy assessed. For example, Hollingsworth and Knight-McKenna (2018), in a small qualitative study with nine pre-service teachers, found that academic service learning with guided reflections before, during and after service improved the teachers' self-efficacy for teaching mathematics. Three recent examples using with purpose-build self-efficacy measurement scales are: Ainscough and colleagues (2016) found that of 850 Australian first-year biology students 81% increased their biology self-efficacy beliefs over the course of one semester, while 16% decreased and 3% remained unchained. In a study of the effects of a 14 week long pedagogical formation education program for 450 Turkish pre-service teachers on their self-efficacy, Berkant & Baysal (2018) found that the pre-service teachers' academic self-efficacy decreased, while their teacher self-efficacy did not change. A most recent study of 96 pre-service teachers participating in a 17-week long assessment course, by Kruse and colleagues (Kruse, Impellizeri, Witherel & Sondergeld, 2020), found that the teachers' assessment self-efficacy increased as a result of the course. Neither of the three studies included investigations of the invariance of the self-efficacy scales used, nor did they include other background factor in their analysis of changes in academic self-efficacy. Palmer's (2006) study on the durability of changes in pre-service teachers' science teaching self-efficacy stands out amongst studies of changes in specific academic self-efficacy, as it documents the

---

[1] APD programs are professionally-oriented higher-education programs combining theoretical studies with a practically oriented approach in the form of mandatory work placement, and they are oriented towards specific professions or job functions (Ministry of Higher Education and Science, 2020). The APD programs are typically two years of length (i.e., 120 ECTS), and are considered level-wise to be equivalent to the first two years of a Bachelor degree.

durability of such changes. Thus, Palmer (2006), in a study of found that the increases in science teaching self-efficacy resulting from participation in a science teaching course were maintained at nine months after the course.

The Current Study

The current study constitutes a first attempt to fill the gap consisting of a lack of knowledge on the relationship between self-efficacy from before starting higher education and across the time span of higher education, by investigating whether later academic self-efficacy can be predicted from pre-academic self-efficacy, while taking into account possible lack of measurement invariance.

Internationally no pre-academic self-efficacy measures have been thoroughly validated using item response theory, and particularly the issue of invariance across programs has not been sufficiently investigated. However, with recent work validating academic self-efficacy scales targeted at the time prior to commencing higher education programs as well as during higher education programs in the Danish context (Nielsen et al., 2017b; Nielsen, 2021a; Nielsen, 2021b), there is a basis for the current study.

Accordingly, the aims of the present work were two-fold: first and primarily, to extend existing knowledge on the relationship between pre-academic self-efficacy and academic self-efficacy during higher education studies. Secondarily, to add to the validity evidence of the PAL-SE and CAL-SE scales, by investigating this for students in teacher education programs[2]. The aims will be achieved through the following research questions:

Primary research question: To what extent can pre-academic self-efficacy of future teacher students predict their academic self-efficacy at the start of the second semester?

In order to answer the primary research question as precisely as possible, a number of secondary research questions will be investigated first.

Secondary research questions:

- Are the items within the PAL-SE and the CAL-SE scales conditionally independent given the latent variable?
- Are measurements by the PAL-SE and the CAL-SE scales invariant and free of differential item functioning (DIF) across student teacher

[2]The teacher education in Denmark is a four-year full-time professional bachelor degree (non-university), which is offered at seven university colleges across the country.

subgroups defined by the university college they attend, gender and age?

- Are the PAL-SE and the CAL-SE scales well-targeted and reliable for the study population of student teachers?

Methods

Instruments

The self-efficacy scales, *Pre-Academic* Learning Self-Efficacy (PAL-SE) and *Current* Academic Learning Self-Efficacy (CAL-SE), employed in the study, are both adaptations of the Specific Academic Learning Self-Efficacy scale (SAL-SE) (Nielsen et al., 2017a).

The SAL-SE scale is a course-specific measure of learning self-efficacy, and one of two subscales derived from the self-efficacy scale in the Motivated Strategies for Learning Questionnaire (MSLQ; Pintrich et al., 1991), using items translated into Danish and an adapted response scale with five categories all with meaning anchors (Nielsen et al., 2017b). The MSLQ is intended to measure students' motivational orientation and learning strategies in high school and higher education (Pintrich et al., 1991), and has been translated into several other languages and is widely used (Credé & Philips, 2011; Duncan & McKeachie, 2005). Initially, the SAL-SE scale was validated for Danish full-program psychology students completing courses in personality psychology, industrial and organisational psychology and biological psychology (Nielsen et al., 2017b). It has since been validated for Danish full-program psychology students completing courses in statistics (Nielsen, 2020), and for Spanish full-program psychology students completing courses in personality psychology, industrial and organisational psychology, biological psychology and research methods (Nielsen, Martínez-García & Alestor, in press 2022)

In the national attrition panel survey (c.f. the section on participants and data collections), from which the data for the present study was drawn, it was not possible to target the specific courses that students were attending, due to the large number of degree programs with different courses. Thus, the learning self-efficacy items was adapted so that instead of referring to "this class/course" as in the SAL-SE and SAE-SE scales, the items referred to "the first courses in my degree program," for the PAL-SE scale and "the current courses in my program" for the CAL-SE scale, while the response categories were not changed (Table A1 in the appendix shows the Danish as well as an English version of the items). Thus, the PAL-SE and CAL-SE scales in this study are not course-specific measures of self-efficacy (as the SAL-SE and the SAE-SE scales), but somewhat more general measures of self-efficacy as they target the first courses students *will be* participating in when they start their programs (PAL-SE), and the courses which they are *currently* participating in (CAL-SE).

The PAL-SE has previously been validated for use with Danish students admitted to nine different university bachelor degree programs across various faculties, all in two universities; medicine, law, psychology, economics, computer science, biology, political science, Danish language, and history (Nielsen et al., 2019), as well as students admitted to 22 different academy profession degree (APD) programs; e.g., APD in financial management, APD in automation technology, APD in optometry (Nielsen 2021a). Nielsen et al., (2019) found that the PAL-SE scale fitted a graphical loglinear Rasch model, which included interaction terms for two locally dependent item pairs (items 1&3 and items 2&4 – the latter being of no consequence) as well as DIF for item 2 relative to the program that students were admitted to. Nielsen (2021a) found that the PAL-SE fitted a somewhat more complicated graphical loglinear Rasch model as this included interaction terms for locally dependent items (items 1&3 and 2&3) as well as DIF for item 3 relative to APD program and item 1 relative to age. The reliability of the PAL-SE for students admitted to university programs ranged from .79 (students admitted to biology) to .86 (students admitted to computer science), with a weighted average across nine programs of .81 (Nielsen et al., 2019). For students admitted to academy profession degree programs, reliability ranged from .66 (APD in Nutrition and technology) to .85 (APD in automation technology) with a weighted average of .77 (Nielsen, 2021a). Targeting of the PAL-SE scale to students admitted to university programs was good with between 73% and 81% of the maximum information obtained (Nielsen et al., 2019). Targeting to students admitted to academy profession degrees on the other hand varied from poor to very good with between 56% and 81% of the maximum information obtained (Nielsen, 2021a). Thus, there is strong evidence across two major education sectors of essential construct validity of the PAL-SE though the scale does function differentially for students admitted to different university and academy profession degrees. Furthermore, the reliability of the PAL-SE has been found to be satisfactory for research purposes, both in the university and academy profession degree context, while the PAL-SE scale is better targeted to students admitted to university than to students admitted to academy profession degree programs.

The CAL-SE has previously been validated for Danish university students in four social science programs each in two universities; Law, Psychology, Economics, and Political Science (Nielsen, 2021b). Nielsen (2021b) found that the CAL-SE fitted a simple graphical loglinear Rasch model as this only included an interaction term for one pair of locally dependent items (items 2&3), and there was no evidence of DIF. Reliability of the CAL-SE for university students in their second semester was .85, and targeting was good with 72% of the maximum information obtained. Thus, there is good initial evidence for the construct validity of the CAL-SE, and both reliability and targeting were good for university students.

Neither the PAL-SE nor the CAL-SE scale has previously been validated for use with students admitted to teacher education programs, and thus this is a necessary step prior to investigating the relationship between PAL-SE and CAL-SE in a longitudinal design.

All items were administered in the same relative order as in the original MSLQ (Pintrich et al., 1991), and they were mixed in with items from other scales not utilized in this study.

Participants and Data Collections

Participants were 407 students admitted to the Danish teacher education program. Participants who completed the PAL-SE scale prior to commencing their studies but after they had been admitted to the teacher education program, and also completed the CAL-SE scale approximately a month into the second semester of the teacher education program. The data were collected by the National Evaluation Institute (EVA) within the framework of their ongoing national longitudinal panel on student attrition. The attrition panel is conducted in the population of students admitted to higher education degree programs through the national Coordinated Admission (KOT) in Denmark. Among students who were admitted to a higher educational program in 2017 a cohort of students participated in a total of four waves of data collection time-wise spanning from admission notice to 13 months after commencing the degree program. Participation was solicited through the national digital mail system in the first wave, where consent was also given. The first wave was collected during two weeks of August after students had received their admittance letter and ending before commencement of the higher education programs in Denmark. The third wave was collected approximately one month into the second semester of study in March. Data for the current study originates from waves one and three for the 2017 cohort, as these included the two scales in question.

The study sample consisted of students admitted across all seven university colleges offering the teacher degree. The mean age of the student was 24.9 years (SD 7.5), and for the purpose of analysis of invariance, the students were divided into four age groups as to have the best possible agreement with the age distribution of all students admitted to the teacher degree program (Table 1). The gender distribution of the study sample was somewhat different than the distribution in all admitted students to the teacher education program, as the study sample only had 29% male students (Table 1).

Table 1. Participant background information used for analyses of differential item functioning (N = 407)

	Study sample		Percentage of all
	Frequency	Percentage	Admitted
Gender			
Male	117	28.8	40.4
Female	209	71.2	59.6
Age groups			
20 years and younger	90	22.1	21.7
21-24 years	207	50.9	49.5
25 years and older	110	27.0	28.8

Statistical Analyses

As no studies had previously validated the scales for use with students in the teacher education program, this was the first step in the analyses. Item analyses were conducted using the Rasch measurement model to establish the construct validity and psychometric properties of both the Pre-Academic Learning Self-Efficacy (PAL-SE) and the Current Academic Learning Self-Efficacy (CAL-SE) scales for teacher students, The resulting interval-scaled estimates of both scale scores were then used in the prediction analysis.

The Rasch Measurement Model

The item analyses were conducted using the Rasch model (RM; Rasch, 1960) in a generalized version for ordinal data known as the Partial Credit Model (PCM; Masters, 1982). As the measurement properties of the RM extend to the PCM, I simply use RM for Rasch model hereafter (Mesbah & Kreiner, 2013). The choice of the RM was made as it is statistically a parsimoneous model describing the causal effect of a latent variable (i.e., the construct measured) on responses to items (i.e., the questions asked) (van der Linden & Hambleton, 1997). The RM is a member of the Item Response Theory (IRT) models with particularly desirable properties (Fischer & Molenaar, 1995; Christensen, Mesbah & Kreiner, 2013), and contrary to other IRT or CFA models, it does not need assumptions on the distribution of the latent variable. The requirements for fit to a Rasch model is (Kreiner, 2013):

1. *Unidimensionality:* The items of the scale should only assess one single underlying latent construct. In this study: the PAL-SE and the CAL-SE scales each assess a unidimensional construct.
2. *Monotonicity:* The expected item scores should increase with increasing values of the latent variable. In this study: the expected score on any PAL-SE item should increase when the total Pre-Academic Learning Self-Efficacy score increases, and the same with the CAL-SE scores.
3. *Local independence of items (no local dependence; no LD):* Responses to items should be *conditionally* independent from the response given to any other item of the same scale given the latent variable. Local independence implies that the response to an item only depends on the level of the construct measured, and not on responses to other items in the scale. In this study, the responses to any of the PAL-SE items should depend only on the level of Pre-Academic Learning Self-Efficacy and not on responses to the other PAL-SE items. Likewise for the CAL-SE items.
4. *Invariance and no differential item functioning (no DIF):* Items and exogenous (i.e., background) variables should be conditionally independent, given the latent variable. Thus, responses to an item must only depend on the level of the construct measured. Gender or other subgroupings of students may have a direct effect on the construct being measured, but the effect on responses to items should be indirectly mediated by the construct. In this study the responses to any of the PAL-SE items should depend only on the level of Pre-

Academic Learning Self-Efficacy and not on any subgroup membership of the students. For example, gender may be directly related to Pre-Academic Learning Self-Efficacy scores, but only related to the item responses trough the scores. Likewise for the CAL-SE items.

5. *Homogeneity:* The ranking of items by the expected item scores should be the same at all levels of the latent variable. In this study: the PAL-SE item requiring the least Pre-Academic Learning Self-Efficacy to be endorsed should be the same item whether students are high or low in Pre-Academic Learning Self-Efficacy, and likewise with the item requiring the most Pre-Academic Learning Self-Efficacy to be endorsed, and so on. The same goes for the CAL-SE scale.

The first four requirements (above) adhere to all parametric and non-parametric IRT models and provide criterion-related construct validity as defined by Rosenbaum (1989). However, the requirement of homogeneity is only satisfied by double monotonic non-parametric IRT models (Mokken, 1971) and by the Rasch model (Rasch, 1960, 1961).

Fulfilment of the five requirements provides: *Score sufficiency* (i.e., the sum score is a sufficient statistic). The property of sufficiency is desirable when using the summed raw score of a scale, as it is the usual case with the PAL-SE and CAL-SE scales. However, fit to the Rasch model also facilitates use of the so-called 'Rasch scores,' which are the person parameter estimates expressed on the logit scale (the distance between any two values on the scale is equal, why this is often referred to as 'interval-scaled scores'). Thus, either the Rasch or the raw sum scores can be used in subsequent analysis, as preferred by the individual researcher or practitioner for their specific purpose. To facilitate such choices, conversion tables between the two will be provided.

Graphical Log-Linear Rasch Models

It is not unusual for measurement scales in education, psychology or the health sciences to be challenged by a lack of conditional independence between items as well as differential item functioning. A classical strategy to resolve issues of local dependence and DIF is to eliminate these items from the scale. However, as scales are often already short and items have been carefully designed to cover sufficient content, such a strategy can be problematic. To avoid eliminating items from already small sets of items, Kreiner &

Christensen (2002, 2004, 2007) proposed a class of extended and generalized Rasch models referred to as graphical log-linear Rasch models (GLLRMs).

In GLLRMs, items can be uniformly locally dependent (i.e., the strength of the association between dependent items is constant across all levels of the latent variable) and items may function differently in different subpopulations defined by background variables if such DIF is also uniform. Rasch models with uniform DIF and uniform LD (GLLRMS) provide essentially valid and objective measurement (Kreiner, 2007a; Kreiner & Christensen, 2007; (Nielsen & Kreiner, 2021, supplemental file 2). The adding of uniform LD and DIF to Rasch models was first proposed by Kelderman (1984). The difference between Kelderman's log-linear Rasch model and GLLRM is that GLLRMs also insert the log-linear Rasch model in a multivariate chain graph model together with background variables and other variables, much in the same way as a CFA can be embedded in a structural equation model (Nielsen & Kreiner, 2021, supplemental file 2).

In chain graph models, nodes are used to represent variables and arrows to illustrate associations among variables. Missing edges or arrows between nodes denote variables that are *conditionally* independent, given the remaining variables in the model. An arrow connecting two variables in a chain graph model may refer to a causal relationship and undirected edges illustrate that the variables are conditionally dependent without causality assumed (Lauritzen, 1996, provides a comprehensive introduction to the theory of graphical models). In GLLRMs the items that are not connected by an edge in a GLLRM graph are conditionally independent given the latent variable (i.e., items are locally independent). Likewise, if there is no arrow or edge between an item and a background variable it means that they are conditionally independent given the latent variable and the other variables in the model. In other words, that there is no DIF. Items are connected to the latent variable to indicate that the relationship is causal. Furthermore, if background variables are directly associated with the latent variable, it may – if the background variable is a criterion variable – indicate that measurement is criterion valid.

Item Analysis by Rasch and Graphical Loglinear Rasch Models

The item analysis included a number of steps in order to rigorously test the fit of the set of items in each scale to the RM or a GLLRM:

- Overall test of homogeneity of item parameters across low and high scoring groups.
- Overall tests of invariance relative to important background variables.

- Tests of no DIF for all items relative to the same background variables.
- Tests of local independence for all item pairs.
- Fit of the individual items to the RM.

The steps were not necessarily taken in the order presented above. For example, if evidence of LD or DIF turned up when testing fit to the RM, log-linear interactions were added to the model and steps repeated until no further evidence against fit of the GLLRM was disclosed.

When the final step had been taken, the analysis was concluded by:

- Assessment of person parameters estimates, standard error and bias of measurement.
- Evaluation of targeting and reliability relative to the current study population.

The overall tests of homogeneity by comparison of item parameters in low- and high-scoring groups and overall tests of invariance were conducted with Andersen's (1973) conditional likelihood ratio test (CLR). The fit of individual items was tested by comparing the observed item-rest-score correlations with the expected item-rest-score correlations under the RM (Kreiner, 2011). Presence of Local Response Dependence (LRD, i.e., positive LD) and DIF in GLLRMs was tested using two tests; tests of conditional independence using partial Goodman-Kruskal gamma coefficients for the conditional association between item pairs (presence of LRD) or between items and exogenous variables (presence of DIF) given scores (Kreiner & Christensen, 2004), and Kelderman's (1984) conditional likelihood ratio test of local independence (LRD and DIF). Specifically, invariance and DIF were tested in relation to gender (male, female), age groups (19 years or younger, 20 years or older), and university college attended (1 to 7). Evidence of fit and no DIF from the overall tests (CLR) was rejected if this was not supported by evidence of individual item fit as well as a lack of evidence of both LD and DIF.

Reliability was estimated with Hamon and Mesbah's (2002) Monte Carlo method for reliability in Rasch scales, as this method can overcome violations of the assumption of conditionally independent items. In contrast, Cronbach's Alpha overestimates the lower bound of reliability if items are locally dependent. Targeting – that is assessment of whether items provide information in the area of the scale where the sample population is located –

was assessed graphically by item maps as well as numerically by two target indices (Kreiner & Christensen, 2013): the test information target index (the mean test information divided by the maximum test information for theta, and the root mean squared error (RMSE) target index (the minimum standard error of measurement divided by the mean standard error of measurement for theta). Both indices should preferably have a value close to one, as this would indicate the degree to which maximum information and minimum measurement error were obtained, respectively). The target of the observed score and the standard error of measurement (SEM) were also estimated. Item maps plot the distribution of the item threshold locations against weighted maximum likelihood estimations of the person parameter locations as well as the person parameters for the population (assuming a normal distribution) and the information function. Critical values were adjusted for false discovery rate (FDR) arising from the multiple statistical tests conducted (i.e., controlling type I errors), whenever appropriate (Benjamini-Hochberg, 1995). As recommended by Cox et al., (1977), the strength of evidence was distinguished as weak ($p <. 05$), moderate ($p < .01$) and strong ($p < .001$) evidence against the model, rather than applying a deterministic 5% critical limit for p-values.

Prediction Analysis

To investigate the primary research question – prediction of the student teacher's academic self-efficacy at the start of the second semester by their pre-academic self-efficacy – general linear models were used for the analysis, as it was then possible to also include background variables such as gender (categorical) and age (continuous) as possible predictors. The person parameter estimates of PAL-SE and CAL-SE resulting from the graphical loglinear Rasch models were rescaled to the range of the raw scores (4.0 to 20.0) and used in the analysis as these are equidistant. PAL-SE was the primary predictor of CAL-SE, while gender, age, university college were secondary predictors. A backwards model-search strategy was employed starting from a model with main effects and all two-way interaction effects, while adhering to the hierarchical principle for exclusion of model components (Kreiner, 2007b).

Software

Item analyses by Rasch models were conducted using DIGRAM (Kreiner, 2003; Kreiner & Nielsen, 2013), item maps were produced in R, while the analysis by general linear models was conducted using SPSS version 26.

Results

Item Analysis

Item analyses of the Pre-Academic Learning Self-efficacy (PAL-SE) scale and the Current Academic Learning Self-Efficacy (CAL-SE) resulted in each scale fitting a graphical log-linear Rasch model (GLLRM) with local response dependence (LRD) between a single item pair in each case (Figure 1). There was no evidence against overall homogeneity or invariance relative to gender, age or university college attended (Table 2), nor was there any evidence of differential item functioning relative to gender, age or university college attended, for the two scales (Appendix Table 2). There was no evidence against the fit of individual items to the GLLRMS for the two scales (Appendix Table 1). In the PAL-SE scale the LRD between items 1 and 3 was medium strong, while the LRD between items 2 and 3 in the CAL-SE scale was very strong, and highly significant, thus necessary to include in the GLLRM (Figure 1, and Appendix Table 3).

Item thresholds and item parameters in the form of location, difficulty, target and information at target are included in Appendix Table 4.

The reliability of both the PAL-SE and the CAL-SE scales was at or above conventional standards of 0.70 for all subgroups of students, with the weighted average across subgroups being 0.73 for the PAL-SE scale and 0.81 for the CAL-SE scale (Appendix Table 5). For the PAL-SE scale reliability varied across subgroups defined by gender and age of the students, with the lowest reliability for female students aged 25 years and older (0.69) and the highest reliability for the youngest and oldest groups – 20 years or below and 25 years or above (0.84). Overall, the reliability of the PAL-SE scale was lower for female than for male students.

Targeting of the PAL-SE scale to the study population was good with more than 75% of the maximum information obtained on average, while the targeting of the CAL-SE scale was somewhat poorer with only 64% of the maximum information obtained (Appendix Table 5). However, when inspecting the item maps in Figure 2, it is evident that even though most information is available at the lower end of each scale (item locations) and the majority of students are located higher on the scales, there is quite high information along the interval of each scale where most students are located and thus targeting is considered sufficient for both scales.

Appendix Table 6 shows the conversion from the summed scale scores to the interval-scaled person parameter estimates resulting from the GLLRMs as well as the rescaled person parameter estimates used in the prediction analysis.

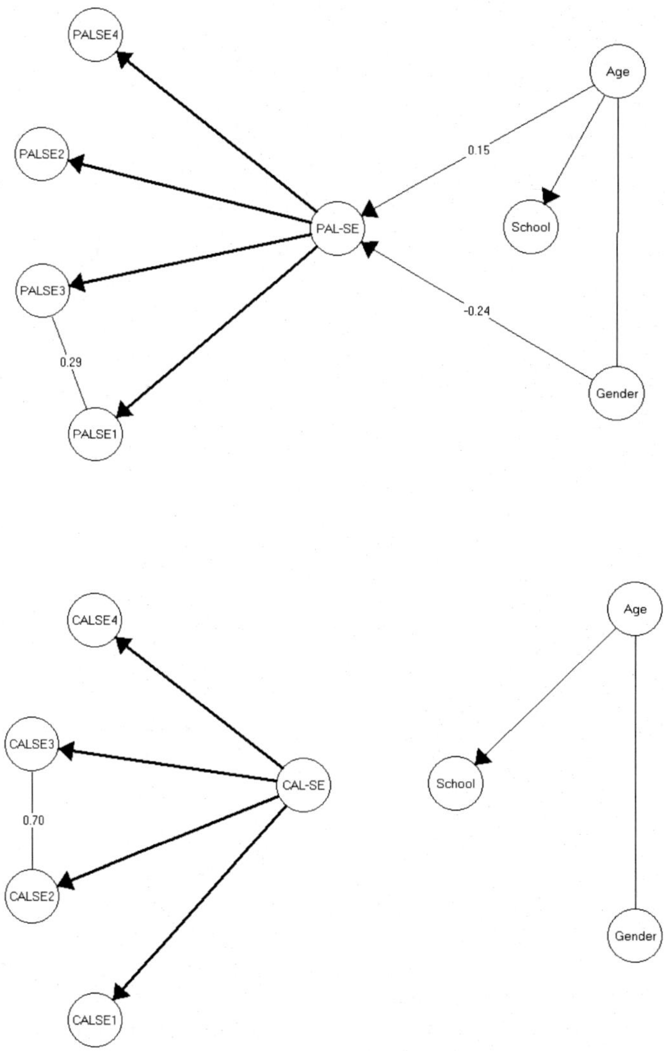

Notes. γ-correlations are partial Goodman and Kruskal's rank correlation for ordinal data. School is university college.

Figure 1. The final Graphical log-linear Rasch models for the Pre-Academic Learning Self-Efficacy Scale (top) and the Current Academic Learning Self-Efficacy scale (bottom).

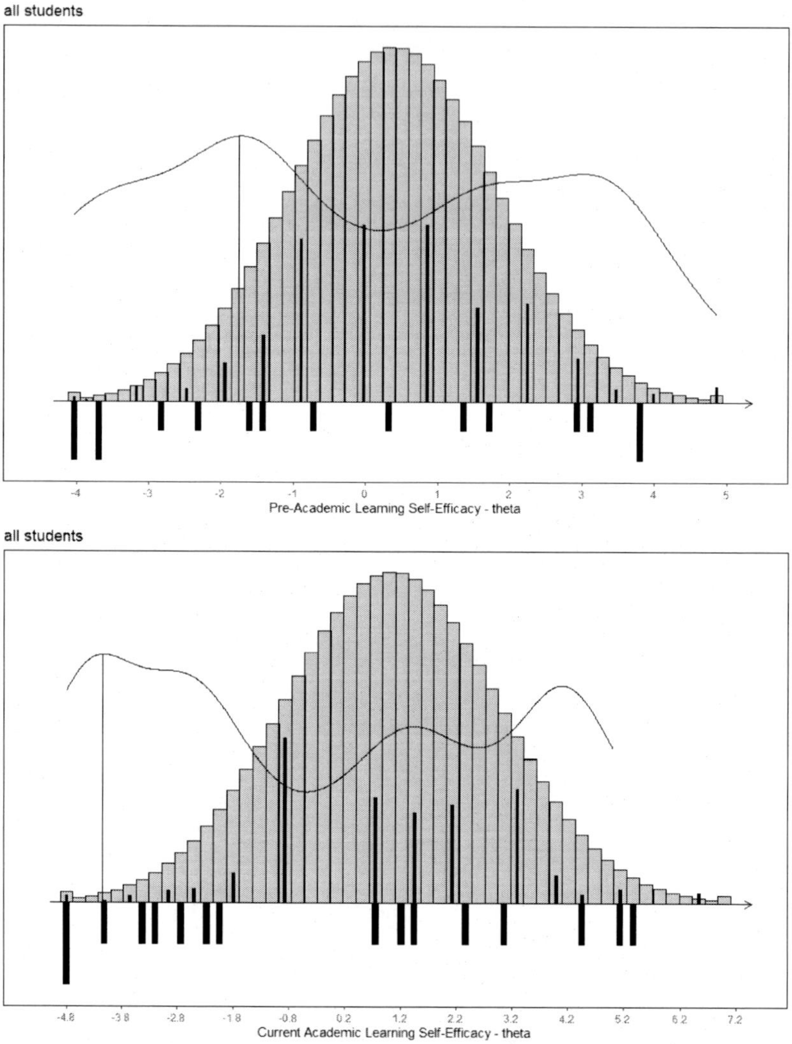

Notes. Person parameters are weighted maximum likelihood estimates and illustrate the distribution of these for the study sample (black bars above the line) and for the population under the assumption of normality (grey bars above the line), as well as the information curve, relative to the distribution of the item thresholds (black bars below the line).

Figure 2. Item maps showing distributions of person parameter estimates and information curve above item threshold locations for the Pre-Academic Learning Self-Efficacy Scale (top) and the Current Academic Learning Self-Efficacy scale (bottom).

Table 2. Global tests of homogeneity and invariance for the Pre-Academic Learning Self-Efficacy and Current Academic Learning Self-Efficacy scales

Tests of fit	PAL-SE RM			PAL-SE GLLRM[a]			CAL-SE RM			CAL-SE GLLRM[b]		
	CLR	df	p	CLR	df	p	CLR	df	p	CLR	df	p
Global homogeneity[c]	20.9	14	.105	20.9	25	.696	58.9	15	.000[++]	41.2	23	.011[+++]
Invariance												
University college	85.6	84	.432	154.4	150	.387	95.2	90	.334	118.1	138	.889
Gender	25.7	14	.028[+]	38.4	25	.042[+]	10.1	15	.814	18.4	23	.736
Age	26.2	28	.560	52.7	50	.370	34.1	30	.277	47.3	46	.420

Notes. PAL-SE = Pre-Academic Learning Self-Efficacy. CAL-SE = Current Academic Learning Self-Efficacy. CLR = Conditional Likelihood Ratio test.

[a] The PAL-SE model assumes that items 1 and 3 are locally dependent.

[b] The CAL-SE model assumes that items 2 and 3 are locally dependent.

[c] The test of homogeneity is a test of the hypothesis that item parameters are the same for persons with low and high scores.

[+] The Benjamini-Hochberg adjusted critical level for false discovery rate at the 5% level was p = .0125 and at the 1% level it was p = .0025.

[++] The Benjamini-Hochberg adjusted critical level for false discovery rate at the 5% level was p = .0500 and at the 1% level it was p = .0100.

[+++] The Benjamini-Hochberg adjusted critical level for false discovery rate at the 5% level was p = .0500 and at the 1% level it was p = .0025.

Prediction of Current Academic Learning Self-Efficacy at the Start of the Second Semester

The result of the analyses with general linear models showed that only *Pre-Academic* Learning Self-Efficacy scores and age predicted *Current* Academic Learning Self-Efficacy scores at the start of the second semester, and only as separate main effects without interaction. Gender and university college did not contribute to the prediction. As both Age and *Pre-Academic* Learning Self-Efficacy scores are continuous variables, the resulting model is, in fact, a multiple linear regression model with both Pre-Academic Learning Self-Efficacy scores and age significantly predicting the Current Academic Learning Self-Efficacy scores a month into the second semester of the teacher education program; $F(2, 404) = 41.333$, $p < .0001$ (Table 3).

PAL-SE contributed most to the prediction of CAL-SE compared to the contribution of age, (see parameter estimates β in Table 3). Furthermore, while PAL-SE scores affect CAL-SE scores positively so that increased PAL-SE scores increase CAL-SE scores, the effect of age is negative so that increased age of the students leads to decreased CAL-SE scores. The predictive contributions of PAL-SE and age are illustrated in Figures XX and YY, In Figure 3 the predicted CAL-SE score is plotted against the PAL-SE scores, while taking into account the effect of age, and as an example it is shown for students at three ages: 19 years, 25 years and 30 years. In Figure 4, the predicted CAL-SE scores are plotted against age, while taking into account the effect of PAL-SE, and as an example it is shown for three different PAL-SE scores. Figure 3 and YY also illustrate that while each of the two predictor variables has an effect on the CAL-SE score, there is no interaction effect between the two as the data lines for the exemplified subgroups are parallel in both cases.

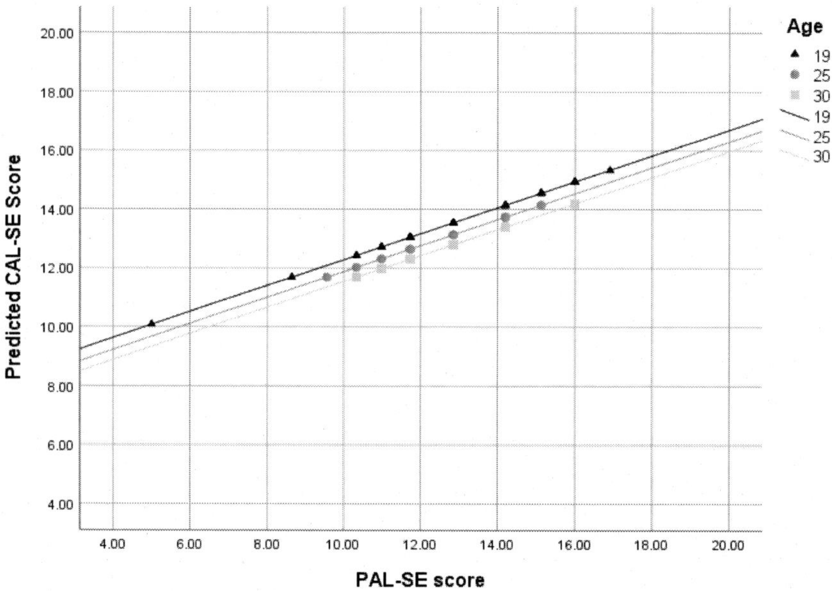

Figure 3. Illustration of the predictive effect of age on CAL-SE scores, while taking into account the effect of PAL-SE, using three ages as examples.

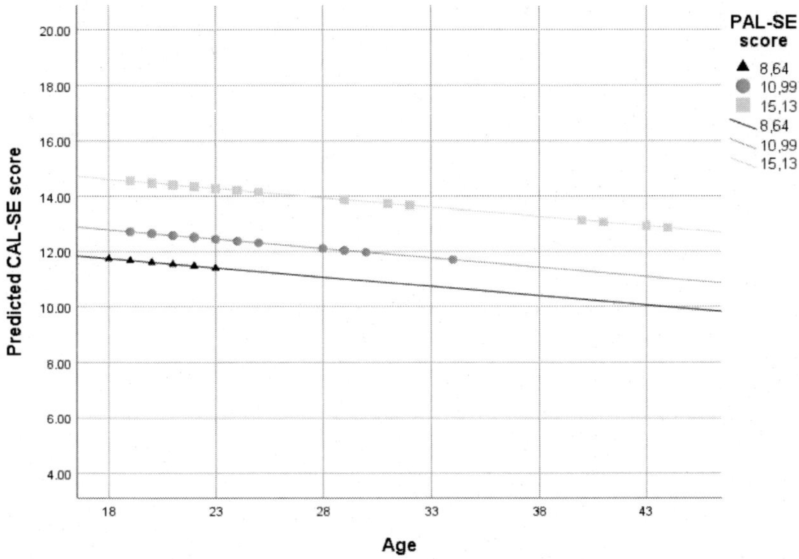

Figure 4. Illustration of the predictive effect of PAL-SE on CAL-SE scores, while taking into account the effect of age, using three selected PAL-SE scores as examples.

Table 3. Parameter estimates for the final multiple linear regression model

	β^a	S.E.	t	p
Predicted CAL-SE score[b]				
Intercept	9.142	0.752	12.159	<.0001
PAL-SE score	0.442	0.052	8.504	<.0001
Age	-0.067	0.015	-4.436	<.0001

Notes. CAL-SE = Current Academic Learning Self-efficacy. PAL-SE = Pre-Academic Learning Self-Efficacy.

[a.] As both predictors are continuous parameter estimates β is only provided as a single value for each predictor.

[b.] Predicted Current Academic Self-efficacy scores for teacher students can be estimated as: CAL-SE score = Intercept + $\beta_{PAL\text{-}SE\ score}$ * PAL-SE score + β_{age} * Age.

Conclusion

The psychometric properties of the PAL-SE and CAL-SE scales students in teacher education programs reported for in this study are comparable to what has been found in previous studies for students admitted to university bachelor program and students admitted to academy profession degree programs

(Nielsen et al., 2019; Nielsen 2021a; Nielsen, 2021b). Thus, while both the PAL-SE and the CAL-SE scales are brief they both fitted simple graphical loglinear Rasch models without any evidence of DIF for the sample of students admitted to the teacher education program. In addition, reliability and targeting of both scales varied across subgroups of students, but were sufficient for the current purpose. Thus, the results of the prediction analysis stand on a firm psychometric foundation and are not biased by lack of invariance or DIF.

The main finding of the study is that both pre-academic learning self-efficacy, as well as age at the time of admission, predicted student teachers' current academic learning self-efficacy six months later. Pre-academic learning self-efficacy contributed the most and positively to current academic learning self-efficacy, while age contributed very little and negatively to the prediction. This adds entirely new knowledge to the field of academic self-efficacy research, as the study is the first to employ a self-efficacy measure targeted to students' beliefs in their ability to learn what is required in their first courses, before they have actually commenced studies to predict scores on a measure targeting students' beliefs in their ability to learn what is required in their second semester courses after having experienced the first semester. However, while the current study shows the predictive value of pre-academic self-efficacy on current academic self-efficacy and controlled for the effects of gender, age, and university college, to be substantial, other predictors might successfully be included in future studies. Likewise, future studies comprising a broader discipline-wise student population, will add further to the field.

In summary, the PAL-SE and the CAL-SE scales can thus be utilized in future studies on changes in academic self-efficacy from prior to commencing studies to later points in studies and how such changes are related to outcomes of higher education. Furthermore, the present study points to a new direction in academic self-efficacy research; namely to uncover how self-efficacy changes and evolves throughout various higher education degree programs using targeted measures, and how longitudinally determined patterns – rather time-point measures – of academic self-efficacy might be associated with educational outcomes.

Acknowledgments

I would like to acknowledge the National Evaluation Institute (EVA) for collecting the data, Morten Rasmus Puck for assisting with the tables,

Christina Lind Donstrup for assisting in searching for literature, and Pedro Henrique Ribeiro Santiago for providing the R-code for the item maps.

References

Ainscough, L., Foulis, E., Colthorpe, K., Zimbardi, K., Robertson-Dean, M. Chunduri, P., & Lluka, L. (2016). Changes in Biology Self-Efficacy during a First-Year University Course. *CBE-Life Sciences Education, 15*, 1-12. https://doi.org/10.1187/cbe.15-04-0092.

Andersen, E. B. (1973). A goodness of fit test for the Rasch model. *Psychometrika*, *38*(1), 123–140. https://doi.org/10.1007/BF022 91180.

Aryee, M. (2017). College students' persistence and degree completion in science, technology, engineering, and mathematics (STEM): The role of non-cognitive attributes of self-efficacy, outcome expectations, and interest (Doctoral dissertation). *ProQuest Dissertations and Theses databases.* (UMI No. 10264673).

Bandura, A. (1997). *Self-efficacy. The exercise of control*. New York: Freeman.

Bartimote-Aufflick, K., Bridgeman, A., Walker, R., Sharma, M., & Smith, L. (2015). The study, evaluation, and improvement of university student self-efficacy. *Studies in Higher Education*, (ahead-of-print), 1-25. https://doi.org/10.1080/03075079.2014.999319.

Benjamini, Y., & Hochberg, Y. (1995). Controlling the False Discovery Rate: A Practical and Powerful Approach to Multiple Testing. *Journal of the Royal Statistical Society. Series B (Methodological)*, *57*(1), 289–300. https://doi.org/10.1111/j.2517-6161.1995.tb02031.x.

Berkant, G. H., & Baysal, S. (2018). An Analysis of the Changes in Pre-Service Teachers' Perceptions towards Teacher Self-Efficacy and Academic Self- Efficacy and their Relations with Several Variables, *International Online Journal of Educational Sciences, 10*(4), 164-182. https://doi.org/10.15345/iojes.2018.04.008.

Burger, K., & Samuel, R. (2017). The Role of Perceived Stress and Self-Efficacy in Young People's Life Satisfaction: A Longitudinal Study. *Journal of Youth and Adolescence, 46* 78–90. http://doi.org/10.1007/ s10964-016-0608-x.

Christensen, K. B., Kreiner, S. & Mesbah, M. (2013). *Rasch models in Health.* London: ISTE & John Wiley & Sons.

Cox, D. R., Spjøtvoll, E., Johansen, S., van Zwet, W. R., Bithell, J. F., Barndorff-Nielsen, O. & Keuls, M. (1977). The Role of Significance Tests [with Discussion and Reply]. *Scandinavian Journal of Statistics*, *4*(2), 49-70. http://www.jstor.org/stable/4615652.

Credé, M., & Phillips, L. A. (2011). A meta-analytic review of the motivated strategies for learning questionnaire. *Learning and Individual Differences, 21*(4), 337–346. http://.doi.org/10.1016/j. lindif.2011.03.002.

De Clercq, M., Galand, B., & Frenay, M. (2017). Transition from high school to university: a person-centered approach to academic achievement. *European journal of psychology of education*, *32*(1), 39-59. http://doi.org/10.1007/s10212-016-0298-5.

Devonport, T. J., & Lane, A. M. (2006). Relationships between self-efficacy, coping and student retention. *Social Behavior and Personality: an international journal*, *34*(2), 127-138. http://doi.org/10.2224/sbp.2006.34.2.127.

Duncan, T. G., & McKeachie, W. J. (2005). The making of the motivated strategies for learning questionnaire. *Educational Psychologist,* *40*(2), 117–128. http://doi.org/10.1207/s15326985ep4002_6.

Elliott, D. C. (2016). The impact of self beliefs on post-secondary transitions: The moderating effects of institutional selectivity. *Higher Education*, *71*(3), 415-431. http://doi.org/10.1007/s10734-015-9913-7.

Ferla, J., Valcke, M., & Cai, Y. (2009). Academic self-efficacy and academic self-concept: Reconsidering structural relationships. *Learning and Individual Differences, 19*(4), 499-505. https://doi.org/ 10.1016/j.lindif.2009.05.004.

Fischer, G. H., & Molenaar, I. W. (Eds.) (1995). *Rasch models – Foundations, recent developments, and applications*. Berlin, Springer-Verlag.

Hamon, A., & Mesbah, M. (2002). Questionnaire reliability under the Rasch model. In M. Mesbah, B. F. Cole & M-LT. Lee. (Eds). *Statistical Methods for Quality of Life Studies.* Dordrecht: Kluwer Academic Publishers, pp. 155-68. http://doi.org/10.1007/978-1-4757-3625-0_13.

Hollingsworth, H. L., & Knight-McKenna, M. (2018) "I am now confident": academic service-learning as a context for addressing math anxiety in preservice teachers. *Journal of Early Childhood Teacher Education,* *39*(4), 312-327. https://doi.org/10.1080/1090 1027.2018.1514337.

Honicke, T., & Broadbent, J. (2015). The influence of academic self-efficacy on academic performance: A systematic review. *Educational Research Review 17*, 63-84. https://doi.org/10.1016/j.edurev. 2015.11.002.

Huang, C. (2013). Gender differences in academic self-efficacy: a meta-analysis. *European Journal of Psychology of Education 28* (1), 1–35. https://doi.org/10.1007/s10212-011-0097-y.

Kelderman, H. (1984). Loglinear Rasch model tests. *Psychometrika, 49*, 223–45. https://doi.org/10.1007/BF02294174.

Kreiner, S. (2003). *Introduction to DIGRAM.* Copenhagen: Department of Biostatistics, University of Copenhagen.

Kreiner, S. (2007a). Validity and objectivity: Reflections on the role and nature of Rasch models. *Nordic Psychology*, *59*, 268 - 298. http://doi.org/10.1027/1901-2276.59.3.268.

Kreiner, S. (2007b). *Statistisk problemløsning. Præmisser, teknik og analyse.* 2. Udgave [*Statistical problem solving. Premises, techniques and analyses*] (2nd ed.). Jurist- og Økonomforbundets forlag.

Kreiner, S. (2011). A note on item-restscore association in Rasch models. *Applied Psychological Measurement*, 35(7), 557–561. https://doi.org/10.1177/014662161141 0227.

Kreiner, S. (2013). The Rasch Model for Dichotomous Items. In Christensen, K. B.; Kreiner, S. & Mesbah, M., (Eds.) *Rasch Models Health.* London, ISTE and John Wiley & Sons, Inc. pp. 5–26. http://doi.org/10.1002/9781118574454.ch1.

Kreiner, S., & Christensen, K. B. (2002). Graphical Rasch Models. In M. Mesbah, B.F. Cole & M-LT. Lee. (Eds). *Statistical Methods for Quality of Life Studies: Design, Measurements and Analysis*. Boston, MA: Springer US, pp. 187–203. http://doi.org/10.1007/978-1-4757-3625-0_15.

Kreiner, S., & Christensen, K. B. (2004). Analysis of local dependence and multidimensionality in graphical loglinear Rasch models. *Communication in Statistics –Theory and Methods, 33*(6), 1239-1276. http://doi.org/10.1081/sta-120030148.

Kreiner, S., & Christensen, K. B. (2007). Validity and objectivity in health-related scales: Analysis by graphical loglinear Rasch models. In M. von Davier & C. H. Carstensen (Eds.), *Multivariate and mixture distribution Rasch models* (pp. 329–346). New York: Springer. http://doi.org/10.1007/978-0-387-49839-3_21.

Kreiner, S., & Christensen, K. B. (2013). Person Parameter Estimation and Measurement in Rasch Models. In Christensen KB, Kreiner S, Mesbah M, (Eds.) *Rasch Models Health.* London, ISTE and John Wiley & Sons, Inc. pp. 63–78. http://doi.org/10.1002/97811185 74454.ch4.

Kreiner, S., & Nielsen, T. (2013). *Item analysis in DIGRAM 3.04. Part I: Guided tours. Research report 2013/06*. University of Copenhagen, Department of Public Health. https://ifsv.sund.ku.dk/biostat/annualreport/images/0/01/ Research_Report_13-06-ny.pdf.

Kruse, L., Impellizeri, W., Witherel, C. E., & Sondergeld, T. A. (2020). Evaluating the Impact of an Assessment Course on Preservice Teachers' Classroom Assessment Literacy and Self-Efficacy. *Mid-Western Educational Researcher, 32*(2), 107 – 132.

Lauritzen, S. L. (1996). *Graphical Models*. Clarendon Press, London.

Lent, R. W., Miller, M. J., Smith, P. E., Watford, B. A., Lim, R. H., & Hui, K. (2016). Social cognitive predictors of academic persistence and performance in engineering: Applicability across gender and race/ethnicity. *Journal of Vocational Behavior*, *94*, 79-88. http://doi. org/10.1016/j.jvb.2016.02.012.

Lindstrøm, C., & Sharma, M. D. (2011). Self-efficacy of first year university physics students: Do gender and prior formal instruction in physics matter? *International Journal of Innovation in Science and Mathematics Education. (formerly CAL-laborate International), 19*(2), 1–19. https://openjournals.library.sydney.edu.au/index.php/ CAL/article/view/4770

Luszczynska, A., Gutiérrez-Doña, B., & Schwarzer, R. (2005). General self-efficacy in various domains of human functioning: Evidence from five countries. *International Journal of Psychology, 40*(2), 80-89. https://doi.org/10.1080/00207590444000041.

Masters, G. N. (1982). A Rasch model for partial credit scoring. *Psychometrika*, 47, 149–174. http://doi.org/10.1007/BF02296272.

Mesbah, M., & Kreiner, S. (2013). The Rasch model for ordered polytomous items. In K. B. Christensen, S. Kreiner & M. Mesbah, (Eds.) *Rasch Models Health.* London, ISTE and John Wiley & Sons, Inc. pp. 27-42. http://doi.org/10.1002/9781118574454.ch2.

Ministry of Higher *Education and Science* (2020). Retrieved July 25th, 2020, from: https://ufm.dk/en/education?set_language=en&cl=en.

Mokken, R. J. (1971) *A theory and procedure of scaler analysis*. Mouton & Co., The Hague.

Multon, K. D., Brown, S. D., & Lent, R. W. (1991). Relation of self-efficacy beliefs to academic outcomes: A meta-analytic investigation. *Journal of counseling psychology, 38*(1), 30-38. http://doi.org/10. 1037/0022-0167.38.1.30.

Muris, P. (2002). Relationships between self-efficacy and symptoms of anxiety disorders and depression in a normal adolescent sample. *Personality and Individual Differences, 32*(2), 337–348. https://doi. org/10.1016/S0191-8869(01)00027-7.

Nielsen, T. (2020). The Specific Academic Learning Self-efficacy and the Specific Academic Exam Self-Efficacy scales: construct and criterion validity revisited using Rasch models. *Cogent Education,* 7(1), 1-15. Article 1840009. http://doi.org/10.1080/2331186X. 2020.1840009.

Nielsen, T. (2021a). Pre-Academic Learning Self-Efficacy revisited: Validation in the Danish Academy Profession Degree context and differences across degree programs. *Scandinavian Journal of Educational Research.* https://doi.org/10.1080/003 13831.2021. 1910559.

Nielsen, T. (2021b). Measuring current academic learning and exam self-efficacy for social science students: a Rasch-based multi degree program validity study. In Braun, E., Esterhazy, R., & Kordts-Freudinger, R. (Eds.) *Research on Teaching and Learning in Higher Education.* Muenster, Germany: Waxmann.

Nielsen, T., Dammeyer, J., Vang, M. L., & Makransky, G. (2017a). Gender fairness in self-efficacy? A Rasch-based validity study of the General Academic Self-efficacy scale (GASE). *Scandinavian Journal of Educational Research,* http://doi.org/10.1080/00313831. 2017.1306796.

Nielsen, T., Friderichsen, I. S., & Hartkopf, B. T. (2019). Measuring academic learning and exam self-efficacy at admission to university and its relation to first-year attrition: an IRT-based multi-program validity study. *Frontline learning Research, 7*(3), 91-118. http://doi. org/10.14786/flr.v7i3.503.

Nielsen, T. & Kreiner, S. (2021). Statistical Anxiety and Attitudes Towards Statistics: criterion-related construct validity of the HFS-R questionnaire revisited using Rasch models. *Cogent Education.* 8 (1), article, 1947941, http://doi.org/10.1080/ 2331186X.2021.1947941.

Nielsen, T., Makransky, G., Vang, M. L. & Dammeyer, J. (2017b): How specific is specific self-efficacy? A construct validity study using Rasch measurement models. *Studies in Educational Evaluation, 57,* 87-97. http://doi.org/10.1016/j.stueduc.2017.04.003.

Nielsen, T., Martínez-García, I., & Alestor, E. (in press). Chapter 5: Psychometric properties of the Spanish translation of the Specific Academic Learning Self-Efficacy and the Specific Academic Exam Self-Efficacy scales in a higher education context. In M. S. Khine & T. Nielsen (Eds.) *Academic Self-efficacy in Education: Nature, Measurement, and Research,* Springer. https://doi.org/10.1080/ 2331186X.2020.1840009.

Pajares, F. (1997). Current directions in self-efficacy research. In M. Maehr & P. R. Pintrich (Eds.), *Advances in motivation and achievement* (Vol. 10, pp. 1–49). Greenwich, CT: JAI Press. https:// www.dynaread.com/current-directions-in-self-efficacy-research.

Palmer, D. (2006). Durability of Changes in Self-efficacy of Preservice Primary Teachers. *International Journal of Science Education, 28*(6), 655-671. https://doi.org/10.1080/09500690500404599.

Pintrich, P. R., Smith, D. A. F., Garcia, T., McKeachie, W. J. (1991). A Manual for the Use of the Motivated Strategies for Learning Questionnaire (MSLQ). *Technical Report No. 91-8-004.* The Regents of The University of Michigan. https://eric.ed.gov/?id=ED338122.

Rasch, G. (1960). *Probabilistic models for some intelligence and attainment tests*. Danish Institute for Educational Research, Copenhagen.

Rasch, G. (1961). *On General Laws and the Meaning of Measurement in Psychology.* The Regents of the University of California. Available from: http://projecteuclid.org/euclid.bsmsp/1200512895.

Richardson, M., Abraham, C., & Bond, R. (2012). Psychological correlates of university students' academic performance: A systematic review and meta-analysis. *Psychological Bulletin*, 138(2), 353. http://dx.doi.org/10.1037/a0026838.

Rosenbaum, P. R. (1989). Criterion-related construct validity. *Psychometrika, 54*, 625 - 633. https://doi.org/10.1007/BF02296400.

Saleh, D., Camart, N., & Romo, L. (2017) Predictors of Stress in College Students. *Frontiers in Psychology, 8*(19). http://doi.org/10.3389/ fpsyg.2017.00019.

Scherbaum, C. A., Cohen-Charash, Y., & Kern, M. J. (2006). Measuring general self-efficacy: A comparison of three measures using item response theory. *Educational and Psychological Measurement*, 66(6), 1047–1063. https://doi.org/10.1177/0013164406288171.

Schunk, D., & Pajares, F. (2002). The development of academic self-efficacy. In A. Wigfield, & J. Eccles (Eds.), *Development of achievement motivation.* San Diego: Academic Press. http://dx.doi. org/10.1016/b978-012750053-9/50003-6.

Tahmassian, K., & Jalali Moghadam, N. (2011). Relationship between self-efficacy and symptoms of anxiety, Depression, worry and social avoidance in a normal sample of students. *Iranian Journal of Psychiatry and Behavioral Sciences, 5*(2), 91–98. https://www.ncbi.nlm.nih.gov/pmc/articles/PMC3939966/.

Thomas, D. (2014). Factors that influence college completion intention of undergraduate students. *The Asia-Pacific Education Researcher*, *23*(2), 225-235. http://doi.org/10.1007/s40299-013-0099-4.

van der Linden, W. J., & Hambleton, R. K. (1997). *Handbook of modern item response theory*. Springer-Verlag, New York. https://doi.org/ 10.1007/978-1-4757-2691-6.

van Herpen, S. G., Meeuwisse, M., Hofman, W. A., Severiens, S. E., & Arends, L. R. (2017). Early predictors of first-year academic success at university: pre-university effort, pre-university self-efficacy, and preuniversity reasons for attending university. *Educational Research and Evaluation, 23*(1-2), 52-72. https://doi.org/10.1080/13803611.2017.1301261.

Vuong, M., Brown-Welty, S., & Tracz, S. (2010). The effects of self-efficacy on academic success of firstgeneration college sophomore students. *Journal of college student development*, *51*(1), 50-64. http://doi.org/10.1353/csd.0.0109.

Yeo, G. B., & Neal, A. (2006). An Examination of the Dynamic Relationship Between Self-Efficacy and Performance Across Levels of Analysis and Levels of Specificity. *Journal of Applied Psychology, 91*(5), 1088 –1101. http://doi.org/10.1037/0021-9010.91.5.1088.

Yong, F. L. (2010). A study on the self-efficacy and expectancy for success of pre-university students. *European Journal of Social Sciences, 13*(4), 514-524.

Young, A. M., Wendel, P. J., Esson, J. M., & Plank, K. M. (2018). Motivational decline and recovery in higher education STEM courses. *International Journal of Science Education*, 40(9), 1016–1033. https://doi.org/10.1080/09500693.2018.1460773.

Zimmerman, B. J., Bandura, A., & Martinez-Pons, M. (1992). Self-motivation for academic attainment: The role of self-efficacy beliefs and personal goal setting. *American educational research journal, 29*(3), 663-676. https://doi.org/10.2307/1163261.

Appendix – Additional Results

Appendix Table 1. Item fit statistics for the Pre-Academic Learning Self-Efficacy and Current Academic Learning Self-Efficacy items

	PAL-SE RM			PAL-SE GLLRM[a]		
items and LRD interaction terms	observed γ	expected γ	p	observed γ	expected γ	p
PAL-SE1	0.70	0.65	.164	0.70	0.69	.756
PAL-SE2	0.57	0.62	.170	0.57	0.59	.647
PAL-SE3	0.73	0.65	.058	0.73	0.70	.511
PAL-SE4	0.59	0.63	.355	0.59	0.60	.926
PAL-SE1*PAL-SE3				0.66	0.61	.206
	CAL-SE RM			CAL-SE GLLRM[b]		
items and LRD interaction terms	observed γ	expected γ	p	observed γ	expected γ	p
CAL-SE1	0.72	0.78	.056	0.72	0.71	.972
CAL-SE2	0.88	0.79	.002[+]	0.88	0.86	.342
CAL-SE3	0.85	0.78	.020[+]	0.85	0.85	.806
CAL-SE4	0.73	0.78	.113	0.73	0.71	.632
CAL-SE2*CAL-SE3				0.77	0.74	.323

Notes. PAL-SE = Pre-Academic Learning Self-Efficacy. CAL-SE = Current Academic Learning Self-Efficacy. γ = Item-restscore correlations for the respective subscale Rasch or graphical log-linear Rasch models in Figure 1 and Table 2. γ-correlations are Goodman and Kruskal's rank correlation for ordinal data. [a] The PAL-SE model assumes that items 1 and 3 are locally dependent. [b] The CAL-SE model assumes that items 2 and 3 are locally dependent. [+] The Benjamini-Hochberg adjusted critical level for false discovery rate at the 5% level was $p = .0333$ and at the 1% level was $p = .0041$.

Appendix Table 2. Conditional likelihood ratio tests of no DIF

DIF terms within subscales	CLR	df	*p*
Pre-Academic Learning Self-Efficacy			
PAL-SE1 & School	18.45	24	.781
PAL-SE2 & School	24.04	24	.460
PAL-SE3 & School	20.47	24	.670
PAL-SE4 & School	25.03	18	.124
PAL-SE1 & Age	6.24	8	.621
PAL-SE2 & Age	0.22	8	.234
PAL-SE3 & Age	10.25	8	.248
PAL-SE4 & Age	3.42		.754
PAL-SE1 & Gender	0.57	4	.970
PAL-SE2 & Gender	13.80	4	.008^{+}
PAL-SE3 & Gender	1.47	4	.833
PAL-SE4 & Gender	5.00	3	.172
Current Academic Learning Self-Efficacy			
CAL-SE1 & School	29.58	24	.199
CAL-SE2 & School	16.14	24	.883
CAL-SE3 & School	19.30	24	.736
CAL-SE4 & School	23.06	24	.516
CAL-SE1 & Age	11.19	8	.191
PAL-SE2 & Age	8.30	8	.404
CAL-SE3 & Age	5.53	8	.700
CAL-SE4 & Age	9.20	8	.326
CAL-SE1 & Gender	0.55	4	.969
CAL-SE2 & Gender	2.27	4	.687
CAL-SE3 & Gender	2.38	4	.667
CAL-SE4 & Gender	2.41	4	.662

Note. γ-correlations are Goodman and Kruskal's rank correlation for ordinal data. $^{+}$ The Benjamini-Hochberg adjusted critical level for false discovery rate at the 5% level was p = .0029.

Appendix Table 3. Conditional likelihood ratio tests of local independence under the two final GLLRMs

LRD terms within scales	CLR	Df	p	γ
Pre-Academic Learning Self-Efficacy				
PAL-SE1 & PAL-SE3	48.33	16	<.0001	0.29
Current Academic Learning Self-Efficacy				
CAL-SE2 & CAL-SE3	82.36	16	<.0001	0.70

Note. γ-correlations are Goodman and Kruskal's rank correlation for ordinal data.

Appendix Table 4. Item thresholds for conditionally independent items and super items made up of locally dependent items

	Thresholds								Location[a]	Item difficulty[b]	Item target[c]	Information at target
items within scales	1	2	3	4	5	6	7	8				
Pre-Academic Learning Self-Efficacy												
PAL-SE2	-3.77	-3.73	-0.64	2.89					-1.31	-2.04	-3.66	0.71
PAL-SE4	---	-2.84	0.27	3.81					0.41	-1.30	0.05	0.32
PAL-SE1*PAL-SE3	-4.66	-2.30	-1.46	-1.52	1.71	1.43	3.81	3.06	0.01	0.08	-1.66	1.14
Current Academic Learning Self-Efficacy												
CAL-SE1	-4.07	-2.25	2.41	5.30					0.35	0.09	-3.13	0.45
CAL-SE4	-5.82	-3.26	0.75	4.47					-0.97	-1.25	-4.27	0.36
CAL-SE2*CAL-SE3	-3.52	-5.35	-2.07	-2.70	1.33	1.29	5.16	3.13	-0.34	-0.62	-4.26	1.01

Notes. --- signifies values not occurring in the data.

[a.] Mean of the thresholds.

[b.] the person parameter where item information is maximized.

[c.] the person parameter where the expected score = max score/2.

Appendix Table 5. Targeting and reliability of the Pre-Academic Learning Self-Efficacy and Current Academic Learning Self-Efficacy scales

	Theta								Score			
Scales and groups defined by variables associated with the scores (n) [a]	target	mean	TI mean	TI max	TI Target index	RMSE mean	RMSE min	RMSE target index	target	mean	mean SEM	r
Pre-Academic Learning Self-Efficacy												
Male, 18-20 years	-1.73	0.78	1.382	1.801	0.767	0.844	0.745	0.883	6.47	14.00	1.17	0.84
Male, 21-24 years	-1.73	0.89	1.379	1.801	0.766	0.852	0.745	0.875	6.47	14.20	1.17	0.72
Male, 25 and older	-1.73	1.07	1.369	1.801	0.760	0.845	0.745	0.881	6.47	14.45	1.16	0.84
Female, 18-20 years	-1.73	-0.19	1.413	1.801	0.784	0.847	0.745	0.879	6.47	12.67	1.19	0.71
Female, 21-24 years	-1.73	0.20	1.393	1.801	0.773	0.851	0.745	0.875	6.47	13.27	1.18	0.72
Female, 25 and older	-1.73	0.43	1.371	1.801	0.761	0.857	0.745	0.870	6.47	13.60	1.17	0.69
Current-Academic Learning Self-Efficacy												
All (no DIF)	-4.13	1.08	1.119	1.746	0.641	0.967	0.757	0.783	3.15	13.74	1.05	0.81

Notes. TI = test information, RMSE = The root mean squared error of the estimated theta score. SEM = The standard error of measurement of the observed score. r = reliability

Targeting and reliability result are provided for subgroups defined by background variables with a significant effect on the respective scale score (c.f. Figure 1).

[a] weighted mean reliability and person separation for the PAL-SE scale: reliability = 0.73, Person separation = 0.75.

Appendix Table 6. Conversion from summed scale scores to weighted maximum likelihood estimates of person parameters and rescaled person parameters for the Pre-Academic Learning Self-Efficacy and Current Academic Learning Self-Efficacy scales

Pre-Academic Learning Self-Efficacy			Current Academic Learning Self-Efficacy		
Summed scale score	Person parameter	Rescaled person parameter	Summed scale score	Person parameter	Rescaled person parameter
4.00	---	---	4.00	-6.832	4.00
5.00	-5.883	5.00	5.00	-5.315	5.82
6.00	-4.554	6.81	6.00	-4.688	6.57
7.00	-3.841	7.77	7.00	-4.199	7.16
8.00	-3.204	8.64	8.00	-3.661	7.80
9.00	-2.528	9.56	9.00	-3.028	8.56
10.00	-1.957	10.33	10.00	-2.458	9.25
11.00	-1.472	10.99	11.00	-1.872	9.95
12.00	-0.932	11.73	12.00	-0.759	11.28
13.00	-0.102	12.85	13.00	0.688	13.02
14.00	0.890	14.20	14.00	1.398	13.87
15.00	1.574	15.13	15.00	2.157	14.78
16.00	2.215	16.00	16.00	3.254	16.10
17.00	2.878	16.90	17.00	3.909	16.88
18.00	3.443	17.67	18.00	4.421	17.50
19.00	4.044	18.49	19.00	5.067	18.27
20.00	5.158	20.00	20.00	6.508	20.00

Notes. Summed scale scores are raw scores. Person parameters are interval-scaled weighted maximum likelihood estimates of the person parameters resulting from the Rasch models. Rescaled person parameters are the WML person parameters rescaled to the original range of the summed raw score, but now interval-scaled.

Chapter 2

Educator Self-Efficacy in Tiered Systems: Theory and Practice

Wendy Peia Oakes[1, *], Kathleen Lynne Lane[2] and Nelson Brunsting[3]
[1]Arizona State University, Mary Lou Fulton Teachers College, Tempe AZ, USA
[2]University of Kansas, School of Education and Human Sciences, Lawrence KS, USA
[3]Wake Forest University, Department of Education, Winston Salem NC, USA

Abstract

Educator wellbeing is promoted when school leaders communicate a clear and sustained vision and provide adequate resources and professional learning opportunities to achieve positive outcomes for students. In this chapter, we provide a theoretical foundation for educator self-efficacy and current empirical evidence exploring self-efficacy of educators who are working in schools implementing tiered systems. We begin with an overview of the theoretical and empirical literature on the importance of educator self-efficacy and wellbeing when engaging in systems efforts. Then, we provide a brief overview of tiered systems. Next, we provide a summary of research conducted to date that examined how teachers fare when working in tiered systems. Then, we discuss core features of tiered systems that promote educators' wellbeing and minimize burnout. We conclude with considerations for educators engaging in system change to promote students' educational outcomes.

Keywords: tiered systems, teacher efficacy, teacher wellbeing, K-12 schools, comprehensive integrated three-tiered model of prevention

[*] Corresponding Author's Email: Wendy.Oakes@asu.edu.

In: The Importance of Self-Efficacy and Self-Compassion
Editor: James J. Carmona
ISBN: 978-1-68507-763-1

The health of a school system, in large part, rests with the wellbeing of its educators (Guin, 2004). Wellbeing is instrumental to educator retention (Billingsley & Bettini, 2019), educators' sense of efficacy (Schussler et al., 2016), and student learning outcomes (Hanushek at al., 2016; Ronfeldt et al., 2013). In this chapter, we provide a theoretical foundation for educator wellbeing and self-efficacy (Bandura, 1993; Rotter, 1966), with attention to empirical evidence exploring wellbeing (e.g., self-efficacy and burnout) of educators working in schools implementing tiered systems (e.g., Lane et al., 2018; McIntosh & Goodman, 2016).

We begin with an overview of the theoretical and empirical literature on the importance of educator self-efficacy and wellbeing for positive teacher and student outcomes (Goddard, Hoy et al., 2000; Wheatley, 2002). Then, we provide a brief overview of tiered systems. Next, we provide a summary of research conducted to date that examined how teachers fare when working in tiered systems. Then, we discuss core features of tiered systems that promote educators' wellbeing and minimize burnout (Menzies, Lane, Oakes, et al., 2020). We conclude with considerations for educators engaging in system change to promote students' educational outcomes.

Educator Self-Efficacy and Wellbeing

Educator self-efficacy has its foundations in social cognitive theory. Bandura (1989) extended prior work on locus of control (RAND, 1970; Rotter, 1966), positing that individuals' behaviors were determined not only by their perception of their ability to act but also by their perceptions of their capability to do so effectively. While individuals can have broad confidence in their abilities, referred to as self-concept, self-efficacy is contextual (Pajares, 1997). For instance, educators may have high self-efficacy for academic instruction in reading and lower efficacy for individualizing instruction based on students' needs. We follow Tschannen-Moran and Woolfolk (2001) in defining educator self-efficacy as an educator's "judgment of [their] capabilities to bring about desired outcomes of student engagement and learning, even among those students who may be difficult or unmotivated" (p. 783). As a construct, educators' sense of efficacy is often measured via the Teacher Self-Efficacy Scale (Tschannen-Moran & Woolfolk Hoy, 2001), which encompasses three areas of teaching: instructional practices, behavior management, and student engagement. More recently, researchers have generated measures to explore other educator self-efficacy domains as well, including self-efficacy for culturally responsive teaching (Siwatu, 2007), self-efficacy for diagnosing student motivational challenges (Hardre & Sullivan, 2008), self-efficacy for integrating technology into instruction (Wang et al., 2004). Research results link educator self-efficacy with a range of important outcomes (Zee & Komen, 2016), including student achievement (Hanushek at al., 2016; Ronfeldt et al., 2013), academic engagement (Sökmen, 2021), and motivation (Lazarides et al., 2018; Mojavezi & Tamiz, 2012). These linkages are often mediated by educators' actions such as the provision of effective feedback (Gibson & Dembo, 1984), time spent on academics (Guo et al., 2012), and use of evidence-based instructional practices (Cumming et al., 2020) to name a few.

In addition to identifying positive outcomes for students, researchers have investigated potential benefits of self-efficacy for educators themselves. A range of research has linked self-efficacy with indicators of educator wellbeing, including emotional exhaustion and burnout (Bettini et al., 2020; Skaalvik & Skaalvik, 2007), stress (Collie et al., 2012), and mental health (Capone & Petrillo, 2020). One commonly-used measure to assess aspects of educators' wellbeing is the Maslach Burnout Inventory—Educators' Scale (MBI-ES; Maslach et al., 1996). Research focused on understanding more specific domains of educator self-efficacy have underscored the connection between educator self-efficacy for managing challenging behaviors and burnout and wellbeing (Garwood et al., 2018; Martin et al., 2012). Although research has begun to examine ways in which educator burnout can grow over time (Brunsting et al., 2021), most studies linking self-efficacy and wellbeing are cross-sectional and in need of longitudinal data to permit fuller examinations of directionality, reciprocity, and impact over time. More recently, researchers have begun to approach educator wellbeing with a focus on positive wellbeing and mental health rather than approaching from challenges in mental health such as burnout and stress. One such approach examines the Dual-Factor Model of Mental Health (Keyes et al., 2012), wherein positive mental health occurs on two axes: mental illness and subjective wellbeing. Teachers with high overall wellbeing experience high subjective wellbeing and low mental illness, while teachers may have mixed levels of overall wellbeing based on various combinations of subjective wellbeing and low mental illness, and low overall wellbeing in times when they report low subjective wellbeing and high mental illness (Fox et al., 2020).

In the next section, we explore tiered systems that hold promise for positive student outcomes and teacher wellbeing.

Tiered Systems

Educational systems adapted tiered systems of prevention from the medical community, as a system-level approach form the early detection and proactive response to students' educational needs (Walker et al., 2004). These systems most often have three tiers of instruction and supports as part of general education. Tier 1 (primary prevention) encompasses educational programming for all students served in the general education context. Tier 1 includes screening practices for the early detection of students with or at risk for learning or behavioral difficulties who may need interventions or supports. Supports are put into place at the earliest sign of concern with students' progress closely monitored. Tier 2 (secondary prevention) encompasses interventions and supports for a smaller group of students (~15%) when data indicate there are addition needs beyond primary prevention efforts need. Tier 2 interventions may be minor adjustments made by the classroom teacher (e.g., targeted use of instructional choice) or small groups classroom-based instruction (e.g., social skills or targeted reading skill groups), as examples. Then, for a few students (~ 5%) with the most intensive needs, Tier 3 interventions are provided (e.g., functional assessment-based interventions; Umbreit et al., 2007). While students with identified disabilities have access to all tiers of interventions and supports within general education as appropriate, special education services are coordinated with but in addition to the tiered levels of supports. Importantly, tiered supports are additive in nature, meaning they supplement but do not replace Tier 1 instruction. As a system-level approach leadership teams, use of data to inform decisions, and professional learning to promote educators use of practices with fidelity are foundation to any tiered system (Lane, Menzies, et al., 2020).

There are multiple system-level tiered models that have differing foci such as Multi-tiered System of Supports (MTSS) where academic and behavioral domains are addressed, Positive Behavioral Interventions and Supports (PBIS; Horner & Sugai, 2002) addressing behavioral and, more recently, social and emotional domains (McIntosh & Goodman, 2016); Response to Intervention (RTI; Fuchs et al., 2003) addressing the academic areas of reading, mathematics, and writing; and the Interconnected Systems Framework (ISF,

Barrett et al., 2012) integrating comprehensive mental health supports and PBIS.

Most recently, there has been a refocusing of efforts to prioritize integrated systems (Institute of Education Sciences [IES], 2018). When implementing an integrated approach, educators work in coordinated ways across special and general education to address students' multiple and complex learning needs across learning domains: academic, behavioral, and social and emotional wellbeing (Lane, Menzies, et al., 2020; McIntosh & Goodman, 2016). The Comprehensive, Integrated Three-tiered (Ci3T) Model of Prevention is one such model designed to comprehensively meet students' needs in all three domains (Lane, Menzies, et al., 2020; Lane & Menzies, 2003; additional details in the next section). In this chapter, we discuss tiered systems generally, and situate illustrations within a Ci3T model of prevention.

Evidence of Educators' Sense of Efficacy and Burnout when Working in Tiered Systems

In the early years of tiered systems inquiry, researchers and practitioners collaborated to determine how implementation of these complex systems occurred with integrity (Buckman et al., 2021) and how student performance academically and behaviorally shifted within and across school years (e.g., Horner & Sugai, 2002; 2015). Progressing from descriptive and correlational studies to randomized controlled trials (e.g., Bradshaw et al., 2012), there is now an extensive body of evidence supporting the efficacy of tiered systems – particularly, PBIS (Lane, Buckman, Oakes, & Menzies, 2021). In addition to these important lessons learned about students fare in tiered systems, there has also been increased attention on how teachers fare in these systems.

Scott Ross was the first scholar to specifically explore the relation between educators' self-efficacy, burnout, and teaching practices in PBIS systems, gleaning findings for inservice and preservice educators. In the first study, Ross and Horner (2007) conducted a pilot study with four schools implementing PBIS, with preliminary findings suggesting a statistically significant relation between educators' self-efficacy ratings and the extent to which PBIS was implemented with integrity. Yet, there was not a significant relation between teacher burnout and PBIS implementation efforts. Shortly afterwards, Ross and colleagues (2012) scaled up this inquiry with a larger sample of 40 elementary schools. Results indicated teachers at schools implementing PBIS with high fidelity reported higher levels of self-efficacy and lower levels of burnout relative to teachers at schools with low levels of PBIS implementation. These first two studies were important in the sense that in addition to PBIS yielding positive outcomes for students, there was also a benefit for the educators themselves.

Oakes, Lane, Menzies, and colleagues recognized the importance of continuing to study educator efficacy in integrated systems as well as for teachers of older students. Specifically, they were interested in examining how teachers fared in Ci3T models: a broadening of MTSS, design to explicitly address students' academic, behavior (PBIS), and social and emotional wellbeing in one integrated system. The Ci3T model is a complex, integrated system in which educators are tasked with multiple responsibilities: utilizing low-intensity supports to increase engagement and minimize disruptions; teaching, practicing, and acknowledging students for using expected behaviors; responding respectfully to challenging behaviors using an established reactive plan for minor and major infractions; and using validated resources to provide instruction in skills needed to support wellbeing (e.g., self-regulation, decision making, self-awareness; Lane, Oakes et al., 2019). These systems require integrated, collaborative efforts between general educators, special educators, mental health providers, administrators, families, and the students themselves. While the building and implementing of integrated systems hold long-term benefits in terms of efficiencies and sustainability, these are indeed complex endeavors (Gandhi et al., 2021).

To explore how educators fare in Ci3T models, Oakes, Lane, and Menzies developed a programmatic line of inquiry dedicated to teacher wellbeing. Oakes et al. (2013) led the first such study at the middle school level during their first year of Ci3T implementation, examining a broader set of variables: (a) treatment integrity and social validity, (b) teacher self-efficacy and burnout, and (c) student behavioral performance according to systematic screening efforts. Results indicated approximately 75% of teachers in the three high-implementing schools reported moderate-to-high levels of emotional exhaustion at the end of the year; yet, more than 90% of teachers reported a strong sense of personal accomplishment. In addition, although still in their first year of implementation, findings were comparable to Ross et al. (2012) results, with educators in high-implementing Ci3T schools reporting lower levels of depersonalization and higher levels of personal accomplished than high-implementing PBIS school. One other noteworthy finding in this preliminary study of how teachers fare in Ci3T middle schools during initial implementation, was that treatment integrity scores predicted depersonalization scores, with teachers reporting higher levels of integrity also experiencing lower levels of depersonalization. This latter finding is particularly encouraging given treatment integrity is a malleable variable that can be enhanced with high-quality professional learning (Lane, Carter et al., 2015; Oakes et al., 2013). Yet, additional questions remained: Were these relations maintained after initial Ci3T implementation (e.g., after two years)? Were these patterns consistent at the elementary and high school levels?

To address these additional studies, Oakes, Menzies, Lane, and colleagues conducted a series of studies funded by an IES practitioner-researcher partnership grant. The research team employed quantitative and qualitative methodologies to determine how elementary (Menzies, Oakes, Lane, Royer, Cantwell, et al., 2021; Oakes, Lane, Royer, et al., 2021) as well as middle and high schools (Lane, Oakes, Royer, et al., 2021; Menzies, Oakes, Lane, Royer, & Buckman, 2021) fare in terms of teachers' wellbeing as measured by self-efficacy (Tschannen-Moran & Woolfolk Hoy, 2001) and burnout (Maslach et al., 1996) after two years of Ci3T implementation.

Educators ($N = 120$) from 14 elementary schools in a Midwestern state in the spring semester of their second year of districtwide Ci3T implementation provided information on self-reports of Ci3T implementation, social validity, as well as efficacy and burnout. Consistent with Oakes et al. (2103) results at the middle school level, elementary educators reported feeling emotionally exhausted. Yet, compared to a national sample, depersonalization and personal accomplishment scores from Ci3T implementers revealed positive and large magnitude differences. During the second year of implementation, elementary educators indicated higher levels of efficacy in instructional strategies and classroom management compared to the national sample. In addition, higher levels of Ci3T treatment integrity were associated with higher sense of self-efficacy related to student engagement. To further understand the meaning elementary teachers made of the Ci3T model and implementation, Menzies and colleagues (2021) invited educators ($N = 18$) from this sample to participate in one of four focus groups. One of the key lessons learned from these studies was that while Ci3T featured three core learning domains: academic, behavior, and social and emotional wellbeing, teachers mainly grappled with students' behavior. More specifically, teachers indicated it was challenging to shift from reactive to proactive classroom management skills theoretically-based in applied behavior analytic principles even as they drew to the end of their second year of implementation. This finding is not entirely surprising given implementation sciences suggests 2-3 years of high-fidelity implementation is often necessary before seeing shifts in desired outcomes (Fixsen et al., 2005). It may be that elementary educators had not experienced the full impact of Ci3T implementation.

Curious as to whether or not middle and high school teachers reported similar experiences after two years of Ci3T implementation as part of the same district-wide initiative, Lane et al. (2021) surveyed 82 middle (4 schools) and high (2 schools) school educators to see how they were faring. Emotional exhaustion ratings were virtually identical to the national sample. Yet, Ci3T implementers reported moderate-to-large positive differences in depersonalization and personal accomplishment scores. In addition, middle and high school educators indicated a higher sense of self-efficacy related to classroom management and instructional strategies relative a national sample. Treatment integrity scores were associated with instructional strategies, student engagement, and classroom management efficacy scores. Currently our research team is analyzing data from two focus groups to understand the meaning secondary teachers made of the Ci3T model and implementation.

Collectively, inquiry to date suggests teachers fare well in tiered systems of support featuring PBIS, with evidence that teachers working in Ci3T systems – although complex – having a higher sense of self-efficacy and lower levels of burnout relative to national norming samples of the tools used. While the business of education may remain emotionally exhausting, it is encouraging to see that high-fidelity implementation of Ci3T is associated with many positive outcomes of educator wellbeing K-12. In the section below, we discuss Ci3T core features that may facilitate teacher wellbeing.

Ci3T Core Features to Facilitate Wellbeing

In the previous section, we explicated the evidence suggesting teachers fare better in schools where they implement tiered models with fidelity, specifically PBIS and Ci3T, compared to teachers from a national sample (Maslach et al., 1996; Tschannen-Moran & Wollfolk Hoy, 2001). In this section, we focus on the following elements that may support teacher wellbeing and are particularly relevant to installing comprehensive reform efforts, such as tiered systems. We feature six elements: (a) clarity of vision and mission, (b) teacher buy-in, (c) role clarity, (d) focused and appropriate professional learning, (e) collaboration and decision making, and (f) use of data. As you will see, there is considerable integration of these elements within tiered systems. We situate the discussion of these elements within the Ci3T model of prevention, illustrating core features of Ci3T that have the potential to support teacher wellbeing.

Clarity of Vision and Mission

Clarity in the administrator's communication of their vision and mission for the school is an active ingredient for building educators' self-efficacy and their willingness to support, or buy in to, a new initiative or comprehensive reform (Turnbull, 2002). Generally, educators have higher job satisfaction and feel more supported in their work when administrators communicate a clear vision for the school, in turn higher efficacy and satisfaction increase educators' persistence in their roles (Sutcher et al., 2016). On the contrary, teachers who do not feel supported by their administrator are two times more likely to leave their positions than those who feel supported (Carver-Thomas & Darling Hammond, 2017).

When schools adopt a Ci3T model of prevention they participate in a year-long design process. School-site Ci3T Leadership Teams, with input from faculty and staff, draft a mission and purpose statement to guide the development of their Ci3T model. That is, they determine the 'why' for engaging in a system-level change effort of adopting a Ci3T model of prevention. Team members capture this vision in their Ci3T mission and purpose statements that is written on the Ci3T primary plan (Lane et al., 2018, 2020; also see ci3t.org/building). Then the team-based approach is used to determine the practices, programs, and strategies to achieve the communicated vision, with multiple opportunities for faculty and staff input throughout the design year. The design year results in the school's full model being made transparent through the use of the Ci3T Implementation Manual – inclusive of the Ci3T Primary (Tier 1) Plan, Reactive Plan, Ci3T Expectation Matrix, Assessment Schedule, Secondary (Tier 2) Intervention Grids, and Tertiary (Tier 3) Intervention Grid. Having everyone on the 'same page,' or clarity in purpose, is often touted by school personnel as a strength of Ci3T (Menzies, Oakes, Lane, Royer, Cantwell, et al. 2021).

A strength of the Ci3T Leadership Team is that they are representative of school and community stakeholders. Team members include at least one administrator, two general education teachers, a special education teacher, one to two other adults (e.g., school counselor, mental health provider, school psychologist), one or two parents, one or two students (the child of the parent member), and a staff member and district Ci3T coach, when possible (Lane, Menzies, et al., 2020). With broad representation, it is more likely that the procedures and practices selected represent the school community and align with the school's mission. Regular and frequent communication between team members and faculty, staff, families, and students, increases the likelihood that stakeholders have opportunities to understand the intended purpose of the reform effort, and contribute their opinions and ideas to the purpose and procedures. Their participation in decisions as to how the model develops contributes to their buy in to the system change effort (Datnow & Castellano, 2000; Menzies, Oakes, Lane, Royer, Cantwell, et al. 2021).

Teacher Buy in

Teacher buy in is often discussed as important for making decisions as to whether to adopt comprehensive system reforms (McDaniel et al., 2017; Turnbull, 2002). However, teacher buy in is a complex construct. Teacher buy in may indicate the alignment of the new practices with the teacher's philosophy, values, beliefs, and experiences (McIntosh et al., 2016), it may also reflect teachers' feelings of efficacy related to new practices. As examples, teachers may ask, "Do I have the skills needed to do this new practice well?" and "Will I be able to help students achieve the desired outcomes?" While evidence suggests teacher buy in is a predictor of immediate and long-term buy in of reform efforts (McIntosh et al., 2016), there are additional considerations.

Some schools choose to use a prespecified criterion for buy in, such as 50% of educators voting in support of adopting a tiered system (e.g., PBIS), to determine sufficient support before moving forward; other times administrators talk informally with educators and staff to assess their acceptability, or buy in, of the reform effort (McIntosh et al., 2016; Turnbull, 2002). However, voting may not be the best indicator of potential success as educators most likely have not had sufficient time to fully understand the 'whys and hows' of the reform effort when the vote is conducted (Turnbull, 2002). Without adequate depth of knowledge about the reform effort, outcomes of the vote may indicate hesitancy of change, feelings of doubt, or other factors. In fact, Wheatley (2002) found that teachers' doubt in their efficacy with specific practices within reform efforts serves to motivate them to engage in professional learning opportunities which are critical to installing reforms, such as Ci3T. So, it is important to ensure all educators and staff have time and opportunities to participate in the design of their tiered system and have access to professional learning opportunities with new practices to increase their understanding of reform efforts, feelings of efficacy and, ultimately, their buy in and implementation.

In the Ci3T model of prevention, school Ci3T Leadership Teams engage in a year-long, six-part professional learning series to design the school's Ci3T plan. The Ci3T design process is data informed, ensuring multiple opportunities for all educators and staff to review and provide feedback on the Ci3T plan as it is developing. By the end of the design year, they have had multiple opportunities to learn about their school's Ci3T model, how it aligns with the school's mission and purpose, and how it will be enacted in their school (e.g., procedures for teaching, reinforcing and monitoring; roles and responsibilities; Lane, Menzies, et al., 2020).

The Primary Intervention Rating Scale (Lane et al., 2002) is used as a formal feedback tool to assess the social validity (i.e., the degree to which stakeholders view the practice to address socially significant goals, socially acceptable procedures, and socially important outcomes; Wolf, 1978) of prevention efforts after educators have the reviewed and discussed the full Tier 1 (primary prevention) plan. In a study by Lane and colleagues (2009), 617 teachers from 19 elementary, middle, and high schools completed the PIRS during their design year. Fourteen of those schools implemented their tiered model in the following school year. Findings suggested PIRS design-year scores predicted Ci3T implementation in their first year as measured by a treatment integrity scale, suggesting a strong relation between social validity during the design year and treatment integrity in the first year of implementation.

During the design year, PIRS data are used by Ci3T Leadership Team members to make refinements to the plan and to determine needed professional learning opportunities prior to and during initial implementation stages. For example, if data indicate educators are not clear on the use of reinforcement, instead of removing that component which is essential to a successful model, the Ci3T Leadership Team would provide professional learning on the foundational principles of Applied Behavior Analysis (ABA) and how reinforcement is instrumental to teaching and promoting students' use of prosocial behaviors (Cooper et al., 2020; Walker et al., 2004). Similarly, the adoption of new assessment tools, such as academic and behavior screeners, require professional learning for teachers to feel efficacious in administering and using the data to inform instructional decisions. A coherent and clear plan allows educators to understand how to be successful in their role in a Ci3T school.

Clarity of Role

In educational systems, there are expected roles for all stakeholders that are determined by larger social expectations of these roles and local context (Richards et al., 2016). Role clarity is when the stakeholder has sufficient information about the responsibilities and expectations for their position to be successful (Brandmo et al., 2019). Research indicates educators' clarity of role is positively related to feelings of autonomy, promotes openness to school reform efforts, and increases efficacy (Brandmo et al., 2019; Gupta, 1981). When there is clarity across roles, and stakeholders generally conform to their expected role, there is likely to be harmony in the system, important for a positive work environment. However, a lack of agreement on role expectations and responsibilities creates tensions and, for educators, can lead to a lower sense of efficacy, overall wellbeing and over time, burnout (Richards et al., 2016).

The adoption of tiered systems has resulted in an expectation of greater coherence across general and special educators for a more seamless system-level approach to prevention and intervention efforts. However, with this expectation comes a change in the previously established roles of teachers which may lead to feelings of ambiguity (Shepard et al., 2016). In a Ci3T model of prevention, there are clarities in the roles and responsibilities of each group of stakeholders: students, faculty and staff, families, and administrators. As part of the Ci3T primary plan, Ci3T Leadership Teams detail the roles and responsibilities for each stakeholder group to achieve their intended purpose and goals across all three learning domains: academic, behavioral, and social and emotional wellbeing.

For educators, responsibilities may include using low intensity strategies during academic lessons to increase student engagement and minimize disruptive behaviors (Lane, Menzies, et al., 2020). For example, such strategies include the use of behavior specific praise (Perez-Clark et al., 2021), precorrection (Sherod et al., 2021), active supervision (Austin et al., 2021), instructional choice (Lane et al., 2021), and opportunities to respond (Haydon et al., 2012; Menzies et al., 2017). Educators are also responsible for conducting accurate and timely assessments such as academic and behavior screening, using data for instructional decision-making, and ensuring the provision of Tier 2 and Tier 3 interventions for students with indicated need. Further, with the adoption of a social skills curriculum as part of their Ci3T model, teachers are expected to teach the lessons according to the schoolwide schedule as well as integrate these lessons throughout the instructional day (Lane, Royer et al., 2021).

Roles and responsibilities described in the school's Ci3T Implementation Manual create transparencies and clarity, not only for teachers but what they can expect of others, which serve to support educator wellbeing. When roles are established, it is important to next consider the professional learning opportunities needed to ensure responsibilities can be met with confidence.

Focused and Appropriate Professional Learning

Educator wellbeing is bolstered when they have appropriate opportunities to gain knowledge and skills to affect positive student outcomes (Armor et al., 1976; Brunsting et al., 2014). As discussed previously, research of tiered models suggests treatment integrity data, the degree to which the plan is implemented as intended (Gresham, 2009) measured at the school (e.g., Ross et al., 2012) and classroom (Lane, Oakes, Royer et al, 2021; Oakes et al., 2021) levels are predictive of teacher efficacy and burnout. Essential to teacher wellbeing and high integrity implementation of practices is appropriate and focused professional learning.

Educators often comment on the disjointed feel of the professional learning offerings within and across school years. The feelings that professional learning does not meet their professional needs may contribute to feelings of conflict (e.g., "Why am I spending time in professional learning on knowledge and skills I already have?") and over time can further exacerbate feelings of burnout (Huberman & Vanderberghe, 1999). High teacher turnover contributes to a sense of unfulfillment in professional learning for experienced teachers who remain (Guin, 2004). This is due to the need for professional learning to focus primarily on new educators to the detriment of experienced educators who already feel confident in more basic knowledge and skills.

However, well-planned professional learning holds many benefits, such as increased use of evidence-based practices to promote student outcomes, high fidelity implementation of practices within the tiered system, as well as increased educator efficacy and decreased burnout, benefiting the whole school community (Geiger & Pivovarova, 2018).

A wealth of evidence suggests teachers do not feel adequately prepared to attend effectively to challenging student behaviors (The New Teacher Report, 2013). Therefore, practice-based professional learning to support teachers in developing the knowledge and skills to effectively manage the classroom and address student behaviors is critical to their long-term persistence in the field (Jennings & Greenberg, 2009). Professional learning for novice teachers might focus on physical room layout, managing paperwork, routines and procedures, and the use of low intensity strategies (Lane, Menzies, et al., 2011). More experienced teachers are likely to have mastered these foundational skills and are more likely to desire deeper levels of learning (Guin, 2004). Therefore, a flexible set of professional learning experiences that promote their high fidelity use practices within their tiered model is needed. Providing a rich selection of professional learning opportunities and resources is warranted. We have learned that educators in Ci3T schools desire choices for professional learning avenues such as: collegial book studies or study groups, district workshops, webinars, brief practice guides, and interactive self-paced learning modules allow teachers to expand and deepen their knowledge and skills through with choice in how and when they engage in these activities (Common et al., 2021; Lane, Carter, et al., 2015; Oakes, Cantwell, et al., 2020). Professional learning in a Ci3T model of prevention attends to the learning of educators and families (see https://www.ci3t.org/) as well as employing a team-based professional learning model to allow time for the review of data, deepening their learning, and strengthening their collaboration to lead their school in implementing and sustaining their Ci3T model.

Collaboration, Autonomy, and Data-Based Decision Making

Supporting educators' wellbeing is a harmonious balance between collaboration and autonomy. Educators often report feeling isolated in their work and challenged to meet all of the needs each of their students (The New Teacher Project, 2013). Collaborative structures can minimize feelings of isolation and educators may feel more supported in meeting students' multiple needs (Ostovar-Nameghi & Sheikhahmadi, 2016). On the other hand, educator autonomy is foundational to educators' sense of efficacy as it is the enactment of agency, the ability to control actions that affect their lives, so, promoting educator autonomy can also improve job satisfaction and efficacy (Zee et al., 2016). Remarkably, when teachers' see students' benefit from a reform effort or new practice, they are more likely to endorse and use the practice even if they feel it impinges on their sense of autonomy (Burns et al., 2013; Datnow & Park, 2019). Educators' use of data for instructional decision-making also may increase their efficacy for meeting students' multiple needs (Datnow & Park, 2019).

Foundational to tiered systems are strong collegial teams and data structures for autonomous decision making. School leadership teams are essential to monitor 'contextual fit' of the school's tiered model (McIntosh et al., 2010, p. 11), guiding each level of implementation and monitoring outcomes (Sugai & Horner, 2006), determining professional learning plans (Sugai & Horner, 2006), and ensuring availability of data for decision making (Lane, Menzies, et al., 2020), with teams' leadership actions (e.g., regular meetings) serving as a predictor of sustainability (McIntosh et al., 2016). Beyond the role of the leadership team are the instrumental functions of grade level teams, department teams, or professional learning communities (PLC; DuFour, 2004) who meet to discuss the implementation of practices, engage in professional learning, and examine data for instructional decision making. Data may also increase teachers' awareness of the importance of high-fidelity implementation to positively affect student achievement (see Buckman et al., 2021).

Collaborative work can be demanding and challenging to initiate (Turnbull, 2002). Recommendations include providing time, resources, and guidance to educators to become effective collaborators (DuFour, 2004). These investments allow for the benefit of distributed leadership empowering educators with opportunities to participate in the regular review of data for decision making, a key variable for increasing teacher efficacy and their support for new reform efforts (Datnow & Castellano, 2000).

Tiered systems rely on the use of data for effective implementation (McIntosh et al., 2013). In fact, use of data also has been found to be an important predictor of the sustainability of tiered systems (McIntosh et al., 2013). Multiple sources of data are collected, analyzed, and used for decision-making. Data are collected on implementation efforts at regular intervals to aid leadership teams in decision making (e.g., Tiered Fidelity Inventory [TFI], Algozzine et al., 2014; Benchmarks of Quality [BOQ], Kincaid et al., 2005; Ci3T Treatment Integrity: Teacher Self-report [Ci3T TI: TSR]; Lane, 2009). In a Ci3T model, all school personnel have an opportunity to reflect on their implementation efforts and report their level of use of specific core practices (e.g., *Do I have the schoolwide expectations posted in my classroom? Do I pair behavior specific praise when giving students PBIS tickets? Am I teaching the social skills lessons according to the school schedule?*) using the Ci3T TI: TSR two times each year (Buckman et al., 2021). Additionally, they complete the PIRS to provide feedback on the social validity of the Ci3T plan at the same two time points. Ci3T Leadership teams review these data and use the information to refine their Ci3T model each summer, inform professional learning plans (Common et al., 2021; Lane, Carter et al., 2015), prompt teacher reflection, and, along with student-level data, select and adopt new practices when needed (e.g., interventions for decreasing disruptive classroom behaviors; Hunter & Haydon, 2019). By completing the surveys, all school personnel can share in the direction of school practices.

The Ci3T Implementation Manual serves to increase transparencies as to expectations, roles and responsibilities, assessment schedules, and available tiered interventions (Lane et al., 2018; 2020). Teachers can, independently or with a professional learning community, use the Ci3T Implementation Manual resources and multiple sources of data to inform instruction. For example, an illustration of the balance between autonomy and collaboration can be illustrated by how teacher use data for making decisions of students' need for Tier 2 and Tier 3 interventions. Having the Ci3T Implementation Manual, documenting all available interventions for a particular school, allows for both autonomous and collaborative decision making. Educators independently review their winter academic and behavioral screening data as well as other important school indicators (e.g., attendance, office discipline referrals, course failures) to determine which students may require a tiered intervention. Then educators can use the Tier 2 or Tier 3 Intervention Grids to select an appropriate intervention given the data indicators (e.g., moderate risk score for externalizing behavior and targeted intervention need in reading fluency). Ci3T tiered intervention grids name and describe each available intervention, list the specific data informed criteria for entry, progress monitoring (e.g., social validity, treatment integrity, and progress monitoring of student performance), and deciding when the student should exit the intervention (Lane, Menzies, et al., 2020). Having these structures in place (i.e., data sources and intervention grids) support educator autonomy without the undue burden of problem solving each unique case without guidance as to appropriate intervention. Likewise, less experienced educators, or those with students who have more intensive needs, may rely on their team to support examining data, selecting and appropriate intervention, and looking at progress data for decisions related to exiting or increasing the intensity of the intervention. Of course, these practices are predicated on the availability of data for decision making.

Considerations for School Leaders Engaging in System Change to Promote Students' Educational Outcomes

When school leaders consider how to engage educators in system-level reform efforts, such as tiered systems, it is important to consider elements found to support adoption efforts such those illustrated by core features of the Ci3T and other tiered models (Turnbull, 2002). In particular, it is important to ensure transparency in communication and structures need to facilitate implementation.

When adopting a tiered model, school leaders are encouraged to articulate their vision and purpose for investing in this school reform effort (Turnbull, 2002). By having clarity of purpose and being able to communicate that message, educators are more likely to understand the 'why' behind the shifts in expectations and practices. This clarity also supports teacher buy in of reform efforts. In addition, a clear vision allows educator to use data to know if they are making progress toward fulfilling this vision. Measures of social validity capture educators' feelings related to the goals, procedures, and outcomes of their tiered model and are a valuable tool for school leaders and leadership teams to monitor any needed adjustments and professional learning (Lane at al., 2009).

Likewise, school leaders ideally have structures in place that clearly detail the roles and responsibilities for all stakeholders. Such clarity promotes educator wellbeing by increasing feelings of being supported by their administrator which in turn serves to decrease feelings of educator burnout and increase persistence (Brandmo et al., 2019; Gupta, 1981; Sutcher et al., 2016). Importantly, teacher self-efficacy and overall wellbeing are related to educators use of evidence-based practices (Cumming et al., 2020) and improvements in student achievement, academic engagement (Hanushek at al., 2016; Ronfeldt et al., 2013; Sökmen, 2021). Therefore, school leaders may want to consider matching learning activities to educators' roles and responsibilities when selecting professional learning. These offering may be more beneficial to educators when they are of appropriate depth for new and experienced teachers

While seemingly simple, providing transparent communication, appropriate professional learning, and ensuring structures to facilitate implementation success are in place, accessed, and evaluated is quite complex. Fortunately, lessons learned today can be used to pave the path for implementation success in a manner that is healthy for students and educators alike.

Conclusion

Inquiry to date indicates school leaders can facilitate educator self-efficacy and well-being by communicating a clear and sustained vision for achieving positive student outcomes, coupled with adequate resources and high-quality professional learning opportunities. In this chapter, we provided a theoretical foundation for educator self-efficacy and current empirical evidence exploring self-efficacy of educators working within tiered systems of support. We began with an overview of the importance of educator self-efficacy when engaging in system reform efforts. Then, we provided a brief overview of tiered systems. Next, we summarized research conducted to date on how teachers fare in tiered systems, noting the role of treatment integrity and social validity of tiered systems. Then, we discussed core features of tiered systems that promote educators' wellbeing and minimize burnout. We concluded with considerations for educators engaging in system change to promote students' educational outcomes.

References

Algozzine, B., Barrett, S., Eber, L., George, H., Horner, R., Lewis, T., Putnam, B., Swain Bradway, J., McIntosh, K. & Sugai, G. (2014). *School-wide PBIS Tiered Fidelity*

Inventory. OSEP Technical Assistance Center on Positive Behavioral Interventions and Supports. www.pbis.org.

Armor, D., Conry-Oseguera, P., Cox, M., King, N., McDonnell, L., Pascal, A., Pauley, E. & Zellman, G. (1976). *Analysis of the school preferred reading program in selected Los Angeles minority schools*. Rand Corporation.

Austin, K. S., Allen, G. E., Brunsting, N. C. & Common, E. A. (2022). Active supervision: Empowering teachers and families to support students in varied learning. *Manuscript in preparation.*

Bandura, A. (1989). Social cognitive theory. In R. Vasta (Ed.), *Annals of child development.* Vol. *6. Six theories of child development* (pp. 1-60). JAI Press.

Bandura, A. (1977). Self-efficacy: Toward a unifying theory of behavioral change. *Psychological Review*, *84*, 191-215. https://doi.org/10.1037/0033-295X.84.2.191.

Bandura, A. (1993). Perceived self-efficacy in cognitive development and functioning. *Educational Psychologist*, *28*, 117–148.

Barrett, S., Eber, L. & Weist, M. D. (2013). *Advancing education effectiveness: An interconnected systems framework for Positive Behavioral Interventions and Supports (PBIS) and school mental health.* Center for Positive Behavioral Interventions and Supports, University of Oregon Press.

Bettini, E., Cumming, M., O'Brien, K. M., Brunsting, N. C., Ragunanthan, M., Sutton, R. & Chopra, A. (2020). Predicting special educators' intent to continue teaching students with emotional/behavioral disorders in self-contained classes. *Exceptional Children*, *86*, 209-228. https://doi.org/10.1177/0014402919873556.

Billingsley, B. & Bettini, E. (2019). Special education teacher attrition and retention: A review of the literature. *Review of Educational Research*, *89*(5), 697-744. https://doi.org/gf5czh.

Bradshaw, C. P., Waasdrop, T. E. & Leaf, P. J. (2012). Effects of school-wide positive behavior interventions and supports on child behavior problems *Pediatrics*, *130*, e1136-e1145.

Brandmo, C., Tiplic, D. & Elstad, E. (2019). Antecedents of department heads' job autonomy, role clarity, and self-efficacy for instructional leadership. *International Journal of Leadership in Education: Theory and Practice*, *3*, 411-430.

Brunsting, N. C., Bettini, E., Rock, M., Royer, D. J., Common, E. A., Lane, K. L., Xie, F., Chen, A. & Zeng, F. (2021). Burnout of special educators serving students with emotional-behavioral disorders: A longitudinal study. *Remedial and Special Education.* https://doi.org/10.1177/07419325211030562.

Brunsting, N. C., Sreckovic, M. A. & Lane, K. L. (2014). Special education teacher burnout: A synthesis of research from 1979 to 2013. *Education and Treatment of Children*, *37*(4), 681-711. https://doi.org/10.1353/etc.2014.0032.

Buckman, M. M., Lane, K. L. & Oakes, W. P. (in press). Treatment Integrity and Social Validity in Tiered Systems: Using Data to Inform Implementation Efforts. In C. J. Lemons, K. L. Lane, S. R. Powell (Eds.). *Handbook of Special Education Research: Research based practices and intervention innovations*. Routledge.

Burns, M. K., Egan, A. M., Kunkel, A. K., McComas, J., Peterson, M. M., Rahn, N. L. & Wilson, J. (2013). Training for generalization and maintenance in RtI implementation:

Front-loading for sustainability. *Learning Disabilities Research & Practice*, *28*(2), 81-88.

Capone, V. & Petrillo, G. (2020). Mental health in teachers: Relationships with job satisfaction, efficacy beliefs, burnout and depression. *Current Psychology*, *39*, 1757-1766. https://doi.org/10.1007/s12144-018-9878-7.

Carver-Thomas, D. & Darling-Hammond, L. (2017). *Teacher turnover: Why it matters and what we can do about it*. Learning Policy Institute. https://learningpolicy institute.org/product/teacher-turnover-report.

Collie, R. J., Shapka, J. D. & Perry, N. E. (2012). School climate and social–emotional learning: Predicting teacher stress, job satisfaction, and teaching efficacy. *Journal of Educational Psychology*, *104*(4), 1189. https://doi.org/10.1037/a0029356.

Common, E. A., Buckman, M. M., Lane, K. L., Oakes, W. P., Royer, D. J., Chafouleas, S., Briesch, A. & Sherod, R. (2021). Project ENHANCE: Assessing Professional Learning Needs for Implementing Comprehensive, Integrated, Three-tiered (Ci3T) Models of Prevention. *Education and Treatment of Children. 44*, 125-144. https://doi.org/10.1007/s43494-021-00049-z.

Cooper, J. O., Heron, T. E. & Heward, W. L. (2020). *Applied behavior analysis* (3rd ed.). Pearson.

Cumming, M., O'Brien, K. M., Brunsting, N. C. & Bettini, E. (2021). Special educators' working conditions, self-efficacy, and instructional and behavior management practice use with students with Emotional/Behavioral Disorders in self-contained settings. *Remedial and Special Education*, *42*, 220-234. https://doi.org/10.1177/0741 932520924121.

Datnow, A. & Park, V. (2019). *Professional collaboration with purpose: Teacher learning for equitable and excellent schools*. Routledge.

Datnow, A. & Castellano, M. (2000). Teachers' responses to Success for All: How beliefs, experiences, and adaptations shape implementation. *American Educational Research Journal*, *37*(3), 775-799. https://doi.org/10.3102/00028312037003775.

DuFour, R. (2004). What Is a "Professional Learning Community"? *Educational Leadership*, *61*, 6-11.

Fixsen, D. L., Naoom, S. F., Blase, K. A., Friedman, R. M. & Wallace, F. (2005). *Implementation research: A synthesis of the literature.* University of South Florida, Louis de la Parte Florida Mental Health Institute, The National Implementation Research Network.

Fox, H. B., Tuckwiller, E. D., Kutscher, E. L. & Walter, H. L. (2020). What makes teachers well? A mixed-methods study of special education teacher well-being. *Journal of Interdisciplinary Studies in Education*, *9*, 223-248. https://doi.org/10.32674/jise.v9i2.

Fuchs, D., Mock, D., Morgan, P. L. & Young, C. L. (2003). Responsiveness-to-intervention: Definitions, evidence, and implications for the learning disabilities construct. *Learning Disabilities Research & Practice*, *18*(3), 157-171.

Garwood, J. D., Werts, M. G., Varghese, C. & Gosey, L. (2018). Mixed-methods analysis of rural special educators' role stressors, behavior management, and burnout. *Rural Special Education Quarterly*, *37*, 30-43. https://doi.org/10.1177/8756870517745270.

Geiger, T. & Pivovarova, M. (2018). The effects of working conditions on teacher retention. *Teachers and Teaching*, *24*(6), 604-625. https://doi.org/djwh

Gibson, S. & Dembo, M. (1984). Teacher efficacy: A construct validation. *Journal of Educational Psychology*, *76*, 569-582.

Gooddard, R. D., Hoy, W. K. & Woolfolk, Hoy, A. (2000). Collective teacher efficacy: Its meaning, measure and student achievement. *American Educational Research Journal*, *37*(2), 479-507.

Gresham, F. M. (1989). Assessment of treatment integrity in school consultation and prereferral intervention. *School Psychology Review*, *18*, 37–50.

Guin, K. (2004). Chronic teacher turnover in urban elementary schools. *Education Policy Analysis Archives*, *12*(42), 1-25. https://doi.org/10.14507/epaa.v12n42.2004.

Guo, Y., McDonald Connor, C., Yang, Y., Roehring, A. D. & Morrison, F. J. (2012). The effects of teacher qualifications, teacher self-efficacy, self-efficacy, and classroom practices on fifth graders' literacy outcomes. *Elementary School Journal*, *113*, 3-24. https://doi.org/10.1086/665816.

Gupta, N. (1981). Some Sources and Remedies of Work Stress among Teachers." (1981). *Southwest Educational Development Laboratory*

Hanushek, E. A., Rivkin, S. G. & Schiman, J. C. (2016). Dynamic effects of teacher turnover on the quality of instruction. *Economics of Education Review*, *55*, 132-148.

Hardré, P. L. & Sullivan, D. W. (2008). Teacher perceptions and individual differences: How they influence rural teachers' motivating strategies. *Teaching and Teacher Education*, *24*(8), 2059-2075.

Haydon, T., MacSuga-Gage, A., Simonsen, B. & Hawkins, R. (2012). Opportunities to respond: A key component of effective instruction. *Beyond Behavior*, *22*(1), 23-31.

Sugai, G. & Horner, R. (2002). The evolution of discipline practices: School-wide positive behavior supports. *Child & Family Behavior Therapy*, *24*(1-2), 23-50.

Horner, R. H. & Sugai, G. (2015). School-wide PBIS: An example of applied behavior analysis implemented at a scale of social importance. *Behavior Analysis in Practice*, *8*(1), 80-85.

Huberman, A. M. & Vandenberghe, R. (1999). Introduction: Burnout and the teaching profession. In R. Vandenberghe & A. M. Huberman (Eds.), *Understanding and Preventing Teacher Burnout: A Sourcebook of International Research and Practice* (pp. 15-37). Cambridge University Press.

Hunter, W. C. & Haydon, T. (2019). Implementing a classroom management package in an urban middle school: A case study. *Preventing School Failure*, *63(1)*, 68-76. https://doi.org/10.1080/1045988X.2018.1504740.

Institute of Education Sciences (2018). *Request for applications: Research networks focus on critical problems of policy and practice in special education* (CFDA 84.324N). U.S. Department of Education.

Jennings, P. A. & Greenberg, M. T. (2009). The prosocial classroom: Teacher social and emotional competence in relation to student and classroom outcomes. *Review of Educational Research*, *79*(1), 491–525. https://doi.org/10.3102/0034654308325693.

Keyes, C. L., Eisenberg, D., Perry, G. S., Dube, S. R., Kroenke, K. & Dhingra, S. S. (2012). The relationship of level of positive mental health with current mental disorders in predicting suicidal behavior and academic impairment in college students. *Journal of American College Health*, *60*(2), 126–133. https://doi.org/10.1080/07448481.2011.608393.

Kincaid, D., Childs, K. & George, H. (2005). *School-wide benchmarks of quality*. Unpublished instrument, University of South Florida.

Lane, K. L., Kalberg, J. R., Bruhn, A. L., Driscoll, S. A., Wehby, J. H. & Elliott, S. (2009). Assessing social validity of school-wide positive behavior support plans: Evidence for the reliability and structure of the Primary Intervention Rating Scale. *School Psychology Review*, *38*, 135–144.

Lane, K. L., Oakes, W. P., Cantwell, E. D. & Royer, D. J. (2018). *Building and installing comprehensive, integrated, three-tiered (Ci3T) models of prevention: A practical guide to supporting school success V1.2.* KOI Education.

Lane, K. L., Robertson, E. J. & Wehby, J. H. (2002). *Primary Intervention Rating Scale.* Rating scale. Available from www.Ci3T.org/measures.

Lane, K. S., Buckman, M. M. & Lane, K. L. (2022). Incorporating choice: Empowering teachers and families to support students in varied learning contexts. *Manuscript in preparation.*

Lane, K. L. (2009). *Comprehensive, Integrated Three-tiered Model of Prevention: Treatment Integrity Teacher Self-Report.* http://www.ci3t.org/measures.

Lane, K. L., Carter, E., Jenkins, A., Magill, L. & Germer, K. (2015). Supporting Comprehensive, Integrated, Three-Tiered Models of Prevention in schools: Administrators' perspectives. *Journal of Positive Behavior Interventions*, *17*, 209–222.

Lane, K. L. & Menzies, H. M. (2003). School-wide intervention with primary and secondary levels of support for elementary students: Outcomes and considerations. *Education and Treatment of Children*, *26*(4). 431-451.

Lane, K. L., Buckman, M. M., Oakes, W. P. & Menzies, H. M. (in press). Tiered systems and inclusion: Potential benefits, clarifications, and considerations. In J. M. Kauffman (Ed.). *On Educational Inclusion: Meanings, History, Issues, and International Perspectives* (pp. 85-106). Routledge Taylor & Francis.

Lane, K. L., Menzies, H. M., Oakes, W. P. & Kalberg, J. R. (2020). *Developing a schoolwide framework to prevent and manage learning and behavior problems* (2nd ed.). Guilford.

Lane, K. L., Oakes, W. P., Royer, D. J., Menzies, H. M., Brunsting, N. C., Buckman, M. M., Common, E. A., Lane, N. A., Schatschneider, C. & Lane, K. S. (2021). Secondary teachers' self-efficacy during initial implementation of comprehensive, integrated, three-tiered models. *Journal of Positive Behavior Interventions*, *23*(4), 232-244. https://doi.org/frdr.

Lane, K. L., Royer, D. J. & Oakes, W. P. (2021). Literacy instruction for students with emotional and behavioral disorders: A developing knowledge base. In R. Boon, M. Burke, and L. Bowman-Perrot (Eds.). *Literacy Instruction for Students with Emotional and Behavioral Disorders (EBD): Research-Based Interventions for the Classroom* (pp. 1-17). Information Age Publishing.

Lane, K. L., Menzies, H., Bruhn, A. & Crnobori, M. (2011). *Managing challenging behaviors in schools: Research-based strategies that work.* Guilford Press.

Lazarides, R., Buchholz, J. & Rubach, C. (2018). Teacher enthusiasm and self-efficacy, student-perceived mastery goal orientation, and student motivation in mathematics classrooms. *Teaching and Teacher Education*, *69*, 1-10. https://doi 10.1016/j.tate.2017.08.017

Martin, N. K., Sass, D. A. & Schmitt, T. A. (2012). Teacher efficacy in student engagement, instructional management, student stressors, and burnout: A theoretical model using in-class variables to predict teachers' intent-to-leave. *Teaching and Teacher Education, 28*(4), 546-559.

Maslach, C., Jackson, S. E. & Leiter, M. P. (1996). *MBI: Maslach burnout inventory*. CPP, Incorporated.

McDaniel, S. C., Kim, S. & Guyotte, K. W. (2017). Perceptions of implementing positive behavior interventions and supports in high-need school contexts through the voice of local stakeholders. *Journal of At-Risk Issues*, *20*(2), 35–44.

McIntosh, K., Mercer, S. H., Hume, A. E., Frank, J. L., Turri, M. G. & Mathews, S. (2013). Factors related to sustained implementation of schoolwide positive behavior support. *Exceptional Children*, *79*(3), 293-311.

McIntosh, K., Mercer, S. H., Nese, R. N. T., Strickland-Cohen, M. K. & Hoselton, R. (2016). Predictors of sustained implementation of school-wide positive behavioral interventions and supports. *Journal of Positive Behavior Interventions*, *18*, 209–218. https://doi.org/10.1177/1098300715599737.

McIntosh, K. & Goodman, S. (2016). *Integrated multi-tiered systems of support: Blending RTI and PBIS.* Guilford Publications.

McIntosh, K., Filter, K. J., Bennett, J. L., Ryan, C. & Sugai, G. (2010). Principles of sustainable prevention: designing scale-up of school-wide positive behavior support to promote. *Psychology in the Schools*, *47*(1), 5-21.

Menzies, H. M., Lane, K. L., Oakes, W. P. & Ennis, R. P. (2017). Increasing students' opportunities to respond: A strategy for supporting engagement. *Intervention in School and Clinic*, *52*(4), 204-209.

Menzies, H. M., Oakes, W. P., Lane, K. L., Royer, D. J. & Buckman, M. M. (2021). Understanding teachers' adoption of a comprehensive reform program. *Manuscript in review.*

Menzies, H. M., Oakes, W. P., Lane, K. L., Royer, D. J., Cantwell, E. D., Common, E. A. & Buckman, M. M. (2021). Elementary teachers' perceptions of comprehensive, integrated three-tiered models of prevention. *Remedial and Special Education*, *42*(4), 207-219. https://doi.org/10.1177/0741932519896860 .

Mojavezi, A. & Tamiz, M. P. (2012). The Impact of Teacher Self-Efficacy on the Students' Motivation and Achievement. *Theory and Practice in Language Studies*, *2*, 483-491. https://doi.org/10.4304/tpls.2.3.483-491.

Oakes, W. P., Cantwell, E. D., Lane, K. L., Royer, D. J. & Common, E. A. (2020). Examining educators' views of classroom management and instructional strategies: School-site capacity for supporting students' behavioral needs. *Preventing School Failure*, *64*(1), 1-11. https://doi.org/10.1080/1045988x.2018.1523125.

Oakes, W. P., Lane, K. L., Jenkins, A. & Booker, B. B. (2013). Three-tiered models of prevention: Teacher efficacy and burnout. *Education and Treatment of Children*, *36*, 95-126.

Oakes, W. P., Lane, K. L., Royer, D. J., Menzies, H. M., Buckman, M. M., Brunsting, N. C., Cantwell, E. D., Schatschneider, C. & Lane, N. A. (2021). Elementary Teachers' self-efficacy during initial implementation of comprehensive, integrated, three-tiered models of prevention. *Journal of Positive Behavior Interventions*, *23*(2), 93-105. https://doi-org./10.1177/1098300720916718.

Ostovar-Nameghi, S. A. & Sheikhahmadi, M. (2016). From teacher isolation to teacher collaboration: theoretical perspectives and empirical findings. *English Language Teaching*, *9*(5), 197-205. http://dx.doi.org/10.5539/elt.v9n5p197.

Pajares, F. (1997). Current directions in self-efficacy research. In M. Maher & P. R. Pintrich (Eds.), *Advances in Motivation and Achievement* (Vol. *10*, pp. 1-50). Emerald Group.

Perez-Clark, P., Royer, D. J. & Gil, H. J. (2022). Behavior-specific praise: Empowering teachers and families to support students in varied learning contexts. *Manuscript in preparation.*

Richards, K., Andrew R., Chantal Levesque-Bristol, Thomas J. Templin, & Kim C. Graber. (2016). "The impact of resilience on role stressors and burnout in elementary and secondary teachers." *Social Psychology of Education*, *19*, no. 3 511-536.

Ronfeldt, M., Loeb, S. & Wyckoff, J. (2013). How teacher turnover harms student achievement. *American Educational Research Journal*, *50*(1), 4–36. https://doi.org/dnb4.

Ross, S. W. & Horner, R. H. (2007). Teacher outcomes of school-wide positive behavior support. *TEACHING Exceptional Children Plus*, *3*(6).

Ross, S. W., Romer, N. & Horner, R. H. (2012). Teacher well-being and the implementation of school-wide positive behavior interventions and supports. *Journal of Positive Behavior Interventions*, *14*(2), 118–128. https://doi.org/10.1177/1098300711413820.

Rotter, J. B. (1966). Generalized expectancies for internal versus external control of reinforcement. *Psychological Monographs*, *80*, 1-28.

Schussler, D. L., Jennings, P. A., Sharp, J. E. & Frank, J. L. (2016). Improving teacher awareness and well-being through care: A qualitative analysis of the underlying mechanisms. *Mindfulness 7*, 130–142. https://doi.org/10.1007/s12671-015-0422-7.

Shepherd, K. G., Fowler, S., McCormick, J., Wilson, C. L. & Morgan, D. (2016). The search for role clarity: Challenges and implications for special education teacher preparation. *Teacher Education and Special Education*, *39*(2), 83-97.

Sherod, R. L., Jones, J. S. & Oakes, W. P. (2021), Precorrection: Empowering teachers and families to support students in varied learning contexts *Manuscript in preparation.*

Siwatu, K. O. (2007). Preservice teachers' culturally responsive teaching self-efficacy and outcome expectancy beliefs. *Teaching and Teacher Education*, *23*, 1086-1101. https://doi.org/10.1016/j.tate.2006.07.011.

Skaalvik, E. M. & Skaalvik, S. (2007). Dimensions of teacher self-efficacy and relations with strain factors, perceived collective teacher efficacy, and teacher burnout. *Journal of Educational Psychology, 99*(3), 611–625. https://doi.org/10.1037/0022-0663.99.3.611.

Sökmen, Y. (2021). The role of self-efficacy in the relationship between the learning environment and student engagement, *Educational Studies*, *47*(1), 19-37, DOI: 10.1080/03055698.2019.1665986.

Sugai, G. & Horner, R. H. (2006). A promising approach for expanding and sustaining school-wide positive behavior support. *School Psychology Review*, *35*, 245-260.

Sutcher, L., Darling Hammond, L. & Carver-Thomas, D. (2016). *A coming crisis in teaching? Teacher supply, demand, and shortages in the U.S.* Learning Policy Institute.

The New Teacher Report (2013). *Teacher Prep Review: A review of the nation's teacher preparation programs. National Council on Teacher Quality.*

Tschannen-Moran, M. & Woolfolk Hoy, A. (2001). Teacher efficacy: Capturing an elusive construct. *Teaching and Teacher Education*, *17*, 783–805.

Turnbull, B. (2002). Teacher participation and buy-in: Implications for school reform initiatives. *Learning Environments Research*, *5*, 235-252. https://doi.org/10.1023/A:1021981622041.

Umbreit, J., Ferro, J., Liaupsin, C. & Lane, K. L. (2007). *Functional behavioral assessment and function-based intervention: An effective, practical approach.* Prentice Hall.

Walker, H. M., Ramsey, E. & Gresham, F. M. (2004). *Antisocial behavior in school: Evidence-based practices* (2nd ed.). Wadsworth Publishing Company.

Wang, L., Ertmer, P. & Newby, T. (2004). Increasing pre-service teachers' self-efficacy beliefs for technology integration. *Journal of Research on Technology in Education*, *36*, 231-252.

Wheatley, K. L. (2002). Teacher persistence: A crucial disposition with implications for teacher education. *Essays in Education*, *3*, 1-13.

Wolf, M. M. (1978). Social validity: The case for subjective measurement or how applied behavior analysis is finding its heart. *Journal of Applied Behavior Analysis*, *11*, 203–214.

Zee, M. & Koomen, H. M. Y. (2016). Teacher self-efficacy and its effects on classroom processes, student academic adjustment, and teacher well-being: A synthesis of 40 years of research. *Journal of Educational Research*, *86*, 981-1015. https://doi.org/10.3102/0034654315626801.

About the Authors

Wendy Peia Oakes, Ph.D., is an associate professor at the Mary Lou Fulton Teachers College at Arizona State University. Her work focuses on practices to improve educational access and outcomes for young children with and at risk for emotional and behavioral disorders. Specifically, her research addresses comprehensive, integrated, three-tiered (Ci3T) models of prevention; the implementation of evidence-based academic and behavioral interventions; and professional development for preservice and in-service educators in implementing practices with fidelity. Dr. Oakes serves as an associate editor for *Remedial and Special Education* and President-elect of the Council for Exceptional Children–Division for Research.

Kathleen Lynne Lane, Ph.D., BCBA-D, CF-L1 is a Roy A. Roberts Distinguished Professor in the Department of Special Education at the University of Kansas and Associate Vice Chancellor for Research. Dr. Lane's research interests focus on designing, implementing, and evaluating comprehensive, integrated, three-tiered (Ci3T) models of prevention to (a) prevent the development of learning and behavior challenges and (b) respond to existing instances, with an emphasis on systematic screening. She is currently past President of the Council for Exceptional Children Division for Research (CEC-DR). She is the co-editor of *Remedial and Special Education.*

Nelson Brunsting, PhD, is the Director of the Center for Research on Abroad and International Student Engagement and a Research Associate Professor of International Studies at Wake Forest University. Dr. Brunsting earned his M.A. in Classics from Victoria University of Wellington, New Zealand, and his PhD in Educational Psychology from the University of North Carolina, Chapel Hill. His research focuses on the wellbeing of diverse populations in academic contexts. He serves on the editorial board of *Remedial and Special Education*.

Chapter 3

Mediated Relationships between Academic Self-Efficacy and Characteristics of Math Performance Differences between Boys and Girls and Students from Immigrant and Non-Immigrant Backgrounds*

Miriam M. Gebauer[1,†]
and Christian Schöber[2]
[1]Ludwig-Maximilian-University, Munich, Germany
[2]Institute for Educational Monitoring and Quality Improvement, Hamburg, Germany

Abstract

Social cognitive learning theory (Bandura, 1997) postulates indirect relations between academic self-efficacy and achievement mediated via persistence. Furthermore, it anticipates reciprocal relations between academic self-efficacy and achievement, but only if scholastic achievement is reported back to the students' and perceived as individual success. The present study examines reciprocal relations between academic self-efficacy and elements of achievement (grades and test results) in math, with persistence as a mediator. It also examines gender differences and differences between students from immigrant and non-

---

* This study was funded by the German Federal Ministry of Education and Research (http://www.bmbf.; grant numbers 01JC1118A and 01JC1118B). The funders had no role in the study design, data collection and analysis, decision to publish, or preparation of the manuscript.

† Corresponding Author's Email: miriam.gebauer@lmu.de.

In: The Importance of Self-Efficacy and Self-Compassion
Editor: James J. Carmona
ISBN: 978-1-68507-763-1

immigrant backgrounds. Data collected from 1,597 students at the beginning of 7th grade and 1,312 at the end were analyzed with bootstrap testing and multigroup structural equation models. Results emphasized the importance of academic self-efficacy for math achievement mediated via persistence. Subgroup-specific results indicate that gender stereotypes and socio-cultural values shape academic self-perceptions.

Keywords: academic self-efficacy, gender differences, mathematics grades, mathematics test scores, persistence, students from immigrant and non-immigrant backgrounds

Introduction

A number of individual and social factors shape students' school performance, and among other self-related beliefs, academic self-efficacy is associated with students' learning behavior and scholastic performance (Bandura, 1997; Dweck, 2002; Pintrich, 2003). This study investigates academic self-efficacy and its meaning for academic performance by addressing three issues: First, as postulated in social cognitive theory, high academic self-efficacy determines school achievement because it encourages students to be more persistent when dealing with demanding tasks (Zimmerman, 2000). Despite abundant research on achievement and academic self-efficacy (e.g., Grigg, Perera, McIlveen, and Svetleff, 2018) as well as on persistence (Bonneville-Roussy, Vallerand, and Bouffard, 2013), the mediated relationship among these three factors has yet to be addressed in detail. Second, social-cognitive learning theory postulates that prior performance also influences later academic self-efficacy, making this is a reciprocal relationship (Pajares and Usher, 2008). However, there is a lack of coherent empirical evidence on this. Recent evidence supports a self-enhancement perspective in which prior mathematic self-efficacy predicts later mathematics achievement (Schöber, Schütte, Köller, McElvany, and Gebauer, 2018; Caprara, Vecchione, Alessandri, Gerbino, and Barbaranelli, 2011). Other studies support a skill-development perspective in which prior learning experience and performance predict later academic self-efficacy (Malmberg and Martin, 2019). One explanation for this lack of coherence could be differences in how achievement is measured. According to social-cognitive theory, achievement explains later academic self-efficacy as long as that achievement is perceived as individual success. This might well be the case for school grades, because these are reported back to students (Bandura, 1997). This raises the question of whether school achievement in math may be more relevant for later academic self-efficacy when measured via school grades than via standardized achievement tests. Third, gender differences and differences between students from immigrant and non-immigrant backgrounds are essential characteristics that need to be taken into account when investigating math achievement and school grades (Höhne and Zander, 2019). Because of the well-known influence of implicitly conveyed gender stereotypes regarding boys' performance and self-referral capabilities in math, boys seem to benefit more from academic self-efficacy (Huang, 2013), whereas girls receive better grades in school at equivalent math performance levels (Neumann, Milek, Maaz, and Gresch, 2010). The second relevant characteristic for students' academic success and academic self-efficacy in this study is cultural diversity due to students' families stemming from different countries and ethnic backgrounds. Research suggests that being raised in differential socio-cultural contexts shapes students' beliefs, understanding and learning behavior (Hofstede, 2001; Minkov et al, 2017), which might be important for the evaluation of perceived school success and, consequently, the formation of academic self-efficacy (McIntyre, Mainhard, and Klassen, 2017).

Self-Efficacy and Persistence

Self-efficacy and persistence are important components of self-regulated learning that are associated with academic performance (Schunk and Usher, 2011). Self-efficacy is described as the perceived belief in one's own capabilities to successfully perform future actions even under challenging conditions (Bandura, 1997). In social cognitive learning theory, self-efficacy is formed through experiences with four *sources*, which describe the processes through which academic self-efficacy develops (Pajares and Usher, 2008): one's own experience, known as *mastery experience*; experiences observed from a model, known as *vicarious experience*; verbal support by a significant other, known as verbal persuasion; and physical sensations perceived in reaction to events, known as *physiological state* (Pajares and Usher, 2008).

Persistence (Feather, 1963), defined as effort and stamina applied to working on a concrete task, is crucial for task performance (Goldhammer et al., 2014). Likewise, achievement is viewed as a function of a person's motivational characteristics, subjectively perceived task difficulty, and the resulting achievement salience (Atkinson, 1957; Atkinson and Feather, 1966). An essential characteristic of goal-oriented action, persistence describes the effort and time spent on pursuing a goal, such as repeating goal attainment processes or trying different approaches to complete a task (Brandstätter, 2014; Liem, Lau, and Nie, 2008). Students with high academic self-efficacy try longer, more often and use alternative solutions to completing a task, whereas students with low self-efficacy give up working on a task more quickly (McFarlin, Baumeister, and Blascovich, 1984). However, by persistently working on tasks, students develop competence (Schunk and Usher, 2011), leading to positive relations between prior grades, academic self-efficacy and persistence (Skaalvik, Federici, and Klassen, 2015).

Persistence can be measured by task completion time (McFarlin et al., 1984) or number of tasks completed or started (Goldhammer et al., 2014). Persistence as time spent on task can be distinguished from general persistence captured by self-statements and self-assessments of one's own action planning and execution, which describe general task-related persistence and endurance in terms of how much effort is put into a task completion process (Dickhäuser, Reinhard, and Englert, 2011). Furthermore, perceived task-related persistence can be distinguished from academic persistence over time, grit (Duckworth and Duckworth, 2016), or anticipated long-term academic goals (Bonneville-Roussy et al., 2013).

Dickhäuser et al. (2011) examined the interaction between certainty and expectancies (certainty × expectancy) and its relation to persistence and math performance in 8th-grade students. They found statistically significant relations between certainty × expectancy and persistence as well as between persistence and performance. Skaalvik et al. (2015) investigated correlations between grades, academic self-efficacy, and persistence. Regression analyses revealed that including academic self-efficacy in the model led the strong statistically significant relation between grades and persistence to vanish.

Despite the large body of research on academic self-efficacy, no study has examined a possible mediated effect of academic self-efficacy via persistence and whether the effect of academic self-efficacy on achievement remains or is completely mediated by persistence.

Math Achievement, Academic Self-Efficacy, and Persistence

Academic self-efficacy is considered a part of educational motivation, which is of substantial importance for scholastic achievement and academic success (Pintrich, 2003; Vollmeyer and Rheinberg, 2000; Wang and Eccles, 2013). A large amount of research investigating the relationship between academic self-efficacy and scholastic achievement emphasizes the strong connection between these two factors (e.g., Parker, Marsh, Ciarrochi, Marshall, and Abduljabbar, 2014).

The literature on the relationship between self-beliefs and achievement reveals three distinguishable positions: the *self-enhancement position*, the *skill development position*, and *reciprocal effect models* (Calsyn and Kenny, 1977). The *self-enhancement position* posits that self-related effectiveness concepts indirectly influence achievement, as they are important for persistence and the learning strategies used (Sedikides and Gregg, 2008). Galla, Wood, Tsukayama, Har, Chiu, and Langer (2014) delivered empirical support for this position by showing that the development of higher levels of academic self-efficacy over time—conveyed through teacher-assessed persistence—influence standardized test scores in math at a later stage. Mittag, Kleine, and Jerusalem (2002) also highlighted the importance of math grades for academic self-efficacy and the significance of academic self-efficacy for school grades measured at a later point in time.

The *skill-development position* sees self-referential effectiveness concepts as outcomes of performance, assuming that a person's educational experiences specifically experiences of school success are reflected in good performance and grades, for example, which in turn further promote the development of academic self-efficacy (Chin and Kameoka, 2002). Malmberg and Martin (2019) found self-sustaining loops in a short-term study investigating within-subject perceived academic performance and academic self-efficacy, thereby indicating the relevance of prior successful learning experiences for later academic self-efficacy.

Reciprocal effect models integrate these two rather opposing positions and assume a reciprocal relationship (Marsh, 1990). Hwang, Choi, Lee, Culver, and Hutchison (2016) found reciprocal relationships between academic self-efficacy and school grades over a five-year period. A meta-analysis found that students' academic self-efficacy was predicted by prior achievement (Talsma, Schütz, Schwarzer, and Norris, 2018). However, these results must be relativized against the background that the meta-analysis combined different school subjects. Schöber et al. (2018) found that the relations seem to differ across subjects, finding reciprocal effects for reading achievement and reading self-efficacy, whereas math self-efficacy predicted later math achievement.

Although grades and achievement tests are both indicators of students' performance, they are based on two different forms of data. Grades are based on assessments of student performance in written and verbal form made by teachers across a number of time points over an entire school year (Duckworth and Seligman, 2006; Faber and Billmann-Mahecha, 2010). Teachers' grading of students' written or verbal performance functions as feedback on individual success and motivation for further accomplishment (Docan, 2006). These teacher evaluations reported back to the students can lead students to perceive success in terms of mastery experiences (Bassi, Steca, Delle Fave, and Caprara, 2007).

To the best of our knowledge, few studies have taken both grades and standardized test results into account. However, the available empirical evidence shows that math self-efficacy is predicted by math grades and test scores over time after controlling for prior math self-efficacy.

Gender Differences

Gender differences in academic self-efficacy occur only in adolescence, in middle and high school, and are usually found in subject and domain-specific self-efficacy, in line with whether the respective subject or domain is more female or male connotated (Huang, 2013). Findings on academic self-efficacy indicate higher levels among girls (Huang, 2013; Vantieghem, Vermeersch, and Van Houtte, 2014). According to Pajares and Valiante (2001), these gender-specific differences cannot be attributed to differential developmental processes, but rather to perceived gender-stereotyped connotations of the subject and domain. Empirical evidence for stereotype activation and corresponding changes in self-efficacy beliefs seems to support this assertion (Wang, Zhou, Tan, and Zhang, 2017).

Although girls seem to outperform boys in many subjects (e.g., Van Houtte, 2004), differences between female and male students in math can still be observed (Husain and Millimet, 2009). Additionally, differences in math performance are attributed to the male connotation of the subject and implicit stereotypes, with empirical findings showing that boys perform better in math than girls (Stoet and Geary, 2013). The number of studies investigating gender differences in academic self-efficacy and academic achievement among students is limited, and not all studies have found gender differences. However, each of these studies used structural equation models to identify differences in response behavior (see Schöber et al., 2018). Explanations for higher grading of girls were attributed to the inclusion of other learning and performance-relevant characteristics of girls in grading or the item formats of standardized test procedures being better suited for boys (Beller and Gafni, 2000; Duckworth and Seligman, 2006).

Differences in Students from Immigrant and Non-Immigrant Backgrounds

In recent years, research has confirmed consistently that students from immigrant backgrounds are disadvantaged compared to their native peers (Ramìrez-Rodrìguez and Dohmen, 2010). Hence, there is a clear need for research on how their learning may function differently and how teaching can adequately respond. Students' social and cultural background shapes their perceptions, beliefs, and learning behavior and form their cultural values. Moreover, social comparisons and anticipated in-group expectations differ between individualist and collectivist cultures (Minkov et al, 2017). Students with more individualist cultural values rate individuality higher, choose downward comparisons and have higher self-beliefs (Minkov et al, 2017). Research points to further differences between students with views shaped by individualist and collectivist cultures, indicating that the former seem to benefit more from perceived success and prior performance (Salili, Chiu, and Lai, 2001). Students of Turkish origin and origins in the former USSR are the largest origin-related subgroups in Germany (Gebhardt, Rauch, Mang, Sälzer, and Stanat, 2013), and both groups are considered to have collectivist views (Minkov et al, 2017). Nevertheless, because students with collectivist views seem to benefit in different ways from prior success, differences between students from immigrant and non-immigrant backgrounds in the relations between academic self-efficacy, persistence, and predicted achievement as measured by grades and test scores can be expected.

The Present Study

Drawing on the aforementioned theoretical frameworks and empirical evidence, this study poses the following research questions:

- *Research question 1.* Is the relationship between academic self-efficacy and performance—measured in terms of both standardized performance tests and grades—mediated via persistence? We expect to find a mediated relationship between academic self-efficacy and achievement (math achievement and grades) via persistence.
- *Research question 2.* Can a relationship between academic self-efficacy and achievement (math achievement and grades) be established from the first to the second measurement point? We expect math self-efficacy to predict math performance at a later point in time. In addition, we expect math grades to predict later academic self-efficacy.

Implicitly conveyed stereotypes regarding mathematics lead to better performance among boys, but on the other hand, students' grades are based on teachers' assessments of learning and performance-relevant behaviour, which leads to better mathematics grades for girls (e.g., Galla et al., 2014). Examining gender differences can provide information on whether girls and boys benefit in different ways from mathematics performance or mathematics grades and from academic self-efficacy and persistence. As a result, the following question will be examined:

- *Research question 3.* Are there differences in the relationships between persistence and achievement (math achievement and grades) between girls and boys? We assume differences in the relationship between academic self-efficacy and math achievement mediated by persistence in favor of boys, because boys outer perform girls in math and thus benefit more from exhibiting persistence. Additionally, we expect differences in the relationship between academic self-efficacy and math achievement as measured by grades mediated by persistence to the disadvantage of boys because grades also implicitly include other aspects relevant to learning and achievement, such as persistence.

In the case of different immigrant subgroups, it can be assumed that Turkish-origin students and students with origins in the former USSR might have fewer experiences of individual ability-related achievement compared to their classmates from non-immigrant backgrounds, because both regions are considered rather collectivist societies.

- *Research question 4.* Can differences be identified between Turkish-origin students, students with origins in the former USSR, and students from non-immigrant backgrounds? We expect differences in favor of students from non-immigrant backgrounds, because students coming from individualist societies are more likely to benefit from their individual experiences of success in terms of their self-related capabilities.

Method

Participants

The sample contained 1,597 students at Time 1 and 1,312 at Time 2 from 71 schools. Data were collected at the beginning (October 2012) and end of 7th grade (June 2013) in the German federal states of North Rhine-Westphalia, Rhineland-Palatinate, Baden-Württemberg, and Lower Saxony. At the beginning of the school year, the students had a mean age of 12.15 years (*SD* = 0.63), and 49.5% were female. Table 1 reports the sample distribution by student subgroup and school type.

Table 1. Students' Distribution in Different School Tracks by Immigrant Subgroup

School track	Family's country of origin	%
Non-academic school track (Hauptschule/Gesamtschule)	Turkey	77.1
	Former USSR	44.0
	Non-immigrant background	37.9
Academic school track (Gymnasium)	Turkey	22.8
	Former USSR	56.0
	Non-immigrant background	62.1

Measures

Mathematics Achievement: Standardized Test Scores

Math performance was assessed with standardized achievement tests (Lehmann, Gänsfuß, and Peek, 1999). These were administered by trained test administrators. Questions addressed the areas of set theory, geometry, and arithmetic. They were presented in multiple-choice or open-answer format. Five plausible values (PV) with a mean value of $M = 100$ ($SD = 30$) were estimated for each study participant.

Mathematics Achievement: School Grades

Students were awarded grades in math by teachers at the end of each grade. For the beginning of the school year, the students' math grades for Grade 6 were used; at the end of the school year, their Grade 7 math grades were available. Grades corresponded to the usual scaling used in Germany of 1 (*very good*) to 6 = (*insufficient*).

Academic Self-Efficacy

Students' academic self-efficacy beliefs were measured with valid methods previously used in other studies (Jerusalem and Satow, 1999; Kunter et al., 2002). Academic self-efficacy was measured with six items rated on a 4-point scale ranging from 1 (*completely disagree*) to 4 (*completely agree*). The global and subgroup reliability was good (see Table 2 and 3). An example item is: "I am certain that I can still reach my desired level of performance in math even if I get one bad grade."

Persistence

Persistence was assessed with six items taken from prior studies (Grob and Maag Merki, 2001). These were rated on a 4-point scale ranging from 1 (*completely disagree*) to 4 (*completely agree*). The construct had good reliability both globally and for the subgroups of interest (see Table 2 and 3). An example item is: "Even when a task is challenging, I will not give up until I am finished."

Target Group Specification

Gender was measured with the two dominant gender categories of female and male (*female* = 2; *male* = 1) based on information provided by the students.[1] Immigrant background was assessed by asking which language was spoken at home and the birthplace of students' parents and grandparents. If both grandparents on one side or one parent was born outside of Germany, the student was categorized as coming from an immigrant background. Data were gathered via student and parent questionnaires. Parent data was taken to be more valid in cases of noncongruence, and student data was used when information from parents was missing.

Control Variables

The first control variable concerned the family's socioeconomic status, measured using the International Socio-Economic Index of Occupational Status (ISEI, Ganzeboom, de Graaf, Treiman, and de Leeuw, 1992). ISEI scores range from 16 to 90, with higher numbers indicating higher status. In cases where both parents were employed, the higher of the parents' two values (HISEI) was used. Data were based on information provided by parents and students. We aggregated both groups of answers. Parent information was considered more valid and student answers were used in the case of missing parent information. The second variable was school type: *Gymnasium*, the academic school track leading to a university entrance qualification; *Hauptschule* and *Realschule*, two school forms leading to vocational education entrance qualifications, and *Gesamtschule*, a school form combining all school tracks. We controlled for *school type* with a coded variable for *Gymnasium* or non-*Gymnasium* (*Gymnasium* = 1; *other school type* = 0).

Data Analysis

Descriptive data analysis and preparation of the data for further analysis were performed using the IBM SPSS program; further analyses were performed

---

[1] At the time the study was conducted, it was usual practice to measure gender with the predominant categories only, not offering further diverse categories.

with M*plus* 8 (Muthén & Muthén, 1998–2018). Achievement data were scaled with item response theory models (Rost, 1996) using ConQuest 3.0 (Adam, Wu, and Wilson, 2012). The number of missing values was between 16.4% and 17.2% for academic self-efficacy (M = 17.3, SD = 0.42) and 18.3% and 19.9% for persistence (M = 19.28, SD = 0.52). Little's (1988) test showed that data were missing completely at random (MCAR, Enders, 2010; Rubin, 1976) for academic self-efficacy (χ^2 = 68.01, df = 72, p = .61) and for persistence (χ^2 = 72.95, df = 70, p = .38). To take missing values into account, we used the FIML setting in M*plus*. We calculated structural equation models with latent variables, setting type = complex to account for the hierarchical structure of the data. We used multigroup structural equation models with latent variables to estimate group comparisons (Brown, 2006). We applied the recommended quality criteria to assess and evaluate each model (Hu and Bentler, 1999) and evaluated the overall model fit with the following four common indices: comparative fit index (CFI), Tucker–Lewis index (TLI), root-mean-square error of approximation (RMSEA), and standardized root-mean-square residual (SRMR). We followed Hu and Bentler's (1999) evaluation criteria (see Table 4 for indices of all models estimated testing for mediation; Table 5 for indices of all models estimated anserwing research questions two, three and four). To examine whether the targeted subgroups could be compared, we examined measurement invariance (MI) for girls compared to boys and for the different origin-related subgroups (Brown, 2006). We used WLSMV estimation and the THETA parameterization to estimate all models, and performed nested model comparisons using the DIFFTEST procedure. No significant differences in the measurement model were found in terms of factor loadings, intercepts, or residuals for either group comparison. We found significant differences in the factor mean and factor variance for the gender-related group comparisons ($\Delta\chi^2$ = 30.95, Δdf = 4, p <. 01) and the origin-related subgroup comparisons ($\Delta\chi^2$ = 36.04, Δdf = 6, p <. 01). We tested the statistical significance of differences between groups in single path coefficients with Wald's test. We also examined whether the relationship between academic self-efficacy and performance was mediated via persistence by testing for mediation with a bootstrap test and confidence intervals in M*plus* (Stride, Gardner, Catley, and Thomas, 2015).

Table 2. Correlations, Means, Standard Deviations, and Reliability of the Total Sample and Immigrant Subgroups

	ASE	PERS	MATH TS	MATH Grade		ASE	PERS	MATH TS	MATH Grade
TP1					TP2				
ASE	-	.46**/.55**	.22**/.25**	-.33**/-.38	ASE	-	.48**/.36**	.25**/.22**	.28**/-.22**
PERS	.46**/.48**	-	.13**/.14	-.19**/-.08	PERS	.50**/.55**	-	.14*/.11	-.21**/-.23**
MATH TS	.28**/.31**	.18**/.31**	-	-.43**/-.45**	MATH TS	.28**/.26**	.14**/.28**	-	-.49**/-.43**
MATH Grade	-.37**/-.39**	-.18**/-.25**	-.51**/-.54**	-	MATH Grade	-.30**/-.39**	-.20**/-.25**	-.49**/-.54**	-
M (SD)					M (SD)				
TURK	2.93 (0.51)	3.00 (0.46)	83.65 (25.10)	3.40 (1.03)	TURK	3.10 (0.57)	3.05 (0.50)	89.95 (24.80)	3.41 (1.02)
SOV	2.92 (0.48)	2.94 (0.50)	104.70 (27.10)	3.10 (1.00)	SOV	3.10 (0.62)	2.93 (0.57)	111.20 (26.30)	3.13 (1.00)
NON	3.10 (0.50)	3.01 (0.51)	113.60 (28.81)	2.84 (1.06)	NON	3.16 (0.56)	3.00 (0.60)	117.30 (28.10)	2.90 (1.10)
ALL	3.00 (0.48)	3.00 (0.49)	100.00 (29.99)	3.10 (1.10)	ALL	3.11 (0.60)	2.20 (0.55)	104.80 (29.40)	3.13 (1.04)
α					α				
TURK	.77	.61	.94		TURK	.82	.68	.90	
SOV	.79	.77	.97		SOV	.86	.81	.90	
NON	.74	.75	.95		NON	.83	.81	.92	
ALL	.76	.70	.96		ALL	.83	.76	.91	

Note: Correlations for students of Turkish (first mention) and USSR heritage (second mention) above the diagonal. Correlations for total sample (first mention) and students from non-immigrant backgrounds (second mention) below the diagonal. ASE = academic self-efficacy; PERS = Persistence; MATH TS = standardized test scores; MATH Grade = school grade in Math; TP1 = Measurement occasion 1; TP2 = Measurement occasion 2; TURK = students' of Turkish heritage; SOV = students' from former state of USSR; NON = students' with no migrant background; ALL = total sample. ** $p < .01$ * $p < .05$.

Table 3. Correlations, Means, Standard Deviations, and Reliability Differentiated for Female and Male Students at Times 1 and 2

	ASE	PERS	MATH TS	MATH Grade		ASE	PERS	MATH TS	MATH Grade
TP1					TP2				
ASE	-	.42**	.24**	-.39**	ASE	-	.43**	.23**	-.34**
PERS	.50**	-	.14**	-.16**	PERS	.50**	-	.14**	-.21**
MATH TS	.31**	.21**	-	-.51**	MATH	.31**	.21**	-	-.48**
MATH Grade	-.36**	-.20**	-.53**	-	MATH Grade	-.27**	-.20**	-.51**	-
M (SD)					M (SD)				
GRL	2.96 (0.50)	2.98 (0.50)	93.90 (29.35)	3.10 (1.04)	GRL	3.10 (0.53)	2.92 (0.53)	100.70 (28.60)	3.13 (1.03)
BOY	3.03 (0.50)	3.01 (0.50)	106.00 (29.41)	3.10 (1.10)	BOY	3.20 (0.61)	3.03 (0.60)	109.10 (29.60)	3.13 (1.10)
α					α				
GRL	.77	.71	.97		GRL	.80	.75	.90	
BOY	.76	.70	.95		BOY	.86	.77	.92	

Note: Correlations for female students above the diagonal and for male students below the diagonal. ASE = academic self-efficacy; PERS = Persistence; MATH TS = standardized test scores; MATH Grade = school grade in Math; TP1 = Measurement occasion 1; TP2 = Measurement occasion 2; GRL = female students; BOY = male students. ** $p < .01$ * $p < .05$.

Table 4. Fit Criteria Mediation Models SEM 01 to SEM 06 for Math Test Scores and Grades

Model	χ^2 (df)	CFI	TLI	RMSEA	SRMR
SEM 01 math test scores	131.77 (43)	.99	.99	.04	.04
SEM 02 math test scores	232.56 (53)	.93	.92	.04	.03
SEM 03 math test scores	312.95 (43)	.98	.99	.06	.07
SEM 04 math test scores	481.25 (116)	.99	.99	.04	.06
SEM 05 math test scores	481.25 (116)	.99	.99	.04	.06
SEM 06 math test scores	693.25 (117)	.98	.98	.05	.07
SEM 01 math grades	63.77 (14)	.97	.96	.04	.03
SEM 02 math grades	45.56 (26)	.93	.92	.05	.04
SEM 03 math grades	35.19 (14)	.98	.95	.04	.02
SEM 04 math grades	173.08 (58)	.99	.99	.04	.06
SEM 05 math grades	173.08 (58)	.97	.95	.03	.04
SEM 06 math grades	300.01 (59)	.93	.91	.05	.04

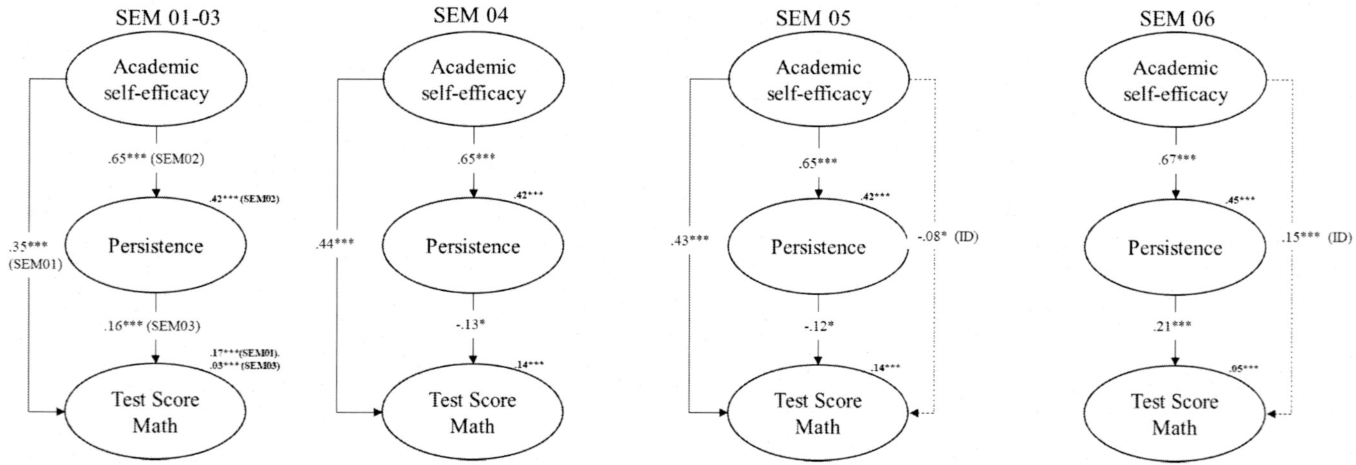

Note: $*p < .05$. $**p < .01$. $***p < .001$.

Figure 1. Mediation analysis of academic self-efficacy via persistence on math test scores.

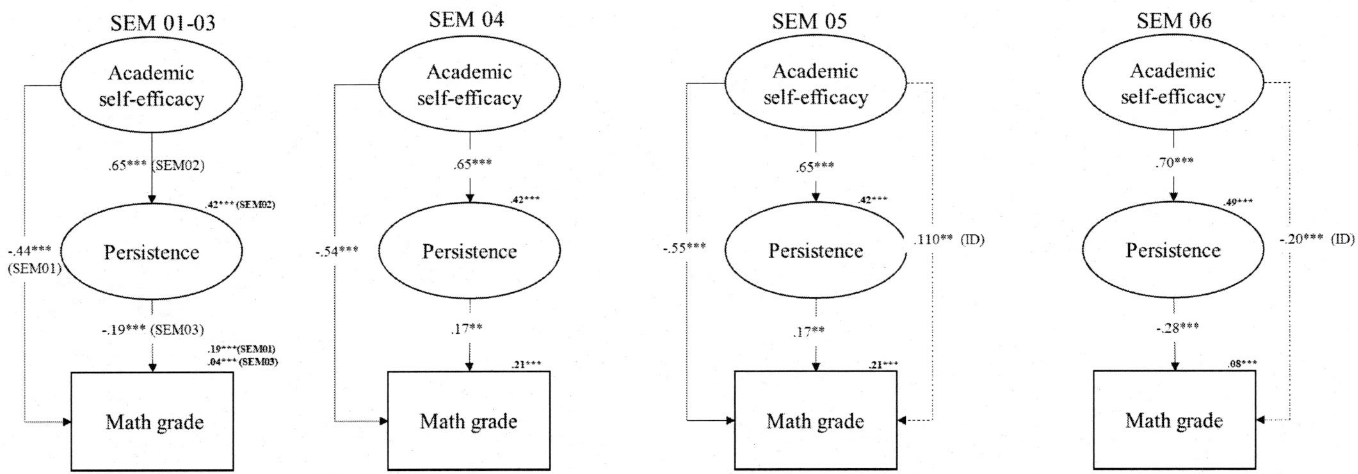

Note: *p < .05. **p < .01. ***p < .001.

Figure 2. Mediation analysis of academic self-efficacy via persistence on math grades.

Table 5. Fit Criteria Mediation Analysis Models illustrated in Figure 3 to Figure 8

Model	χ^2 (df)	CFI	TLI	RMSEA	SRMR
Mediation analysis of academic self-efficacy via persistence on math test scores over time	1827.03 (518)	.97	.97	.04	.07
Mediation analysis of academic self-efficacy via persistence on math grades over time	9337.43 (325)	.93	.92	.04	.05
Mediation analysis of academic self-efficacy via persistence on math test scores over time among female and male students	2593.23 1302.53/1290.7a (1224)	.96	.96	.04	.09
Multi-group structural mediation model of academic self-efficacy via persistence on math grades over time among female and male students	1540.45/818.20/ 722.25a (670)	.91	.91	.04	.07
Multi-group structural mediation model of academic self-efficacy via persistence on math test scores over time among students from immigrant and non-immigrant backgrounds	5001.55/1104.78/835.06/ 1191.25 b (3144)	.95	.95	.04	.09
Multi-group structural mediation model of academic self-efficacy via persistence on math grades over time among students from immigrant and non-immigrant backgrounds	2607.59/553.99/434.29/ 624.94 b (1720)	.91	.90	.04	.07

Note: a First mentioned χ^2 for all students, second for female students and third for male students; b First mentioned χ^2 for all students, second for Turkish-origin students, third for students from the former USSR, fourth for students from non-immigrant backgrounds.

Results

Mediation Analysis

We applied a systematic stepwise analysis to test for mediation (see Figures 1 and 2: models SEM 01 to SEM03) and then estimated all path coefficients simultaneously in a single model to analyze the relationship between academic self-efficacy, persistence, and standardized test scores; and again in a single model explaining school grades in math (see Figure 1 [test scores model] and Figure 2 [school grades model]: model SEM 04 simultaneously considering all path coefficients). Results of bootstrap tests for indirect-only effects revealed a statistically significant effect of academic self-efficacy with confidence intervals from .09 to .18 for the model using standardized test scores (see Figure 1 [test scores model]: SEM 06 for all path coefficients and Table 4 for model fit criteria). When testing indirect-only effects between academic self-efficacy and school grades in math via persistence assuming completely indirect effects, confidence intervals were -.29 to .12 (see Figure 2 [school grades model]: SEM 06 for all path coefficients and Table 4 for model fit criteria). When including direct path coefficients between math achievement in two models, one with test scores and one with school grades as the outcome of interest, there were unexpected negative path coefficients between persistence and achievement (test scores and school grades) indicating theoretically unexpected competitive mediation (Zhao, Lynch Jr, and Chen, 2010). Nevertheless, bootstrap tests of competitive mediation models for test scores and school grades showed significant indirect effects with confidence intervals from .60 to .72.

Testing Relationships over Time

The indirect-only model for Time 1 was extended to include an indirect-only model for Time 2—once with math achievement assessed via test scores and another based on school grades. When considering Time 1 and Time 2 simultaneously (see Figure 3 [test scores model] and Figure 4 [school grades model] as well as Table 5 for model fit criteria), the mediated relationship between academic self-efficacy and achievement via persistence remained for Time 1 but could no longer be found for Time 2. Furthermore, the coefficients

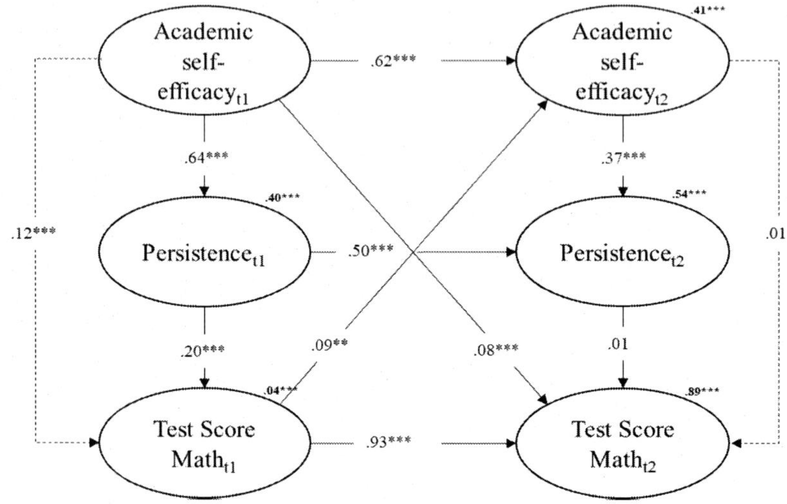

Note: t1 = measurement occasion 1; t2 = measurement occasion 2. *$p < .05$. **$p < .01$. ***$p < .001$.

Figure 3. Mediation analysis of academic self-efficacy via persistence on math test scores over time.

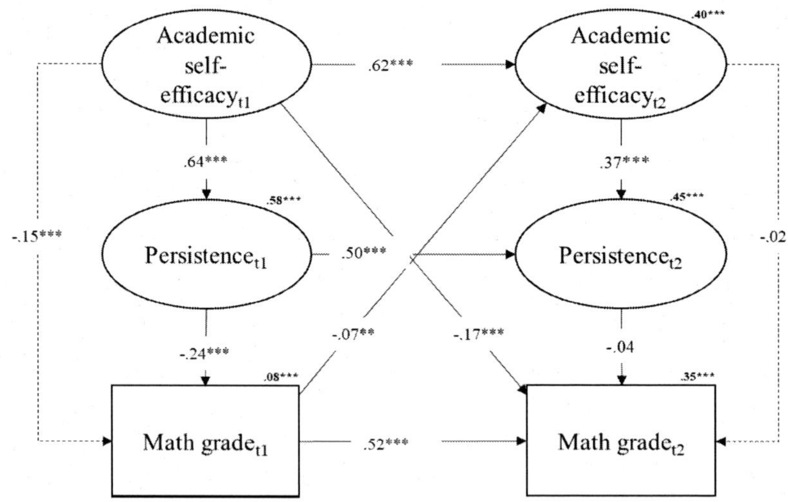

Note: t1 = Measurement point one, t2 measurement point two. *$p < .05$. **$p < .01$. ***$p < .001$.

Figure 4. Mediation analysis of academic self-efficacy via persistence on math grades over time.

between academic self-efficacy and persistence remained statistically significant at both time points. However, a statistically significant path coefficient between persistence and achievement characteristics (test scores and school grades) could be observed only for Time 1. This might have been due to high path coefficients for achievement variables measured at Time 1 explaining performance at Time 2.

There were only small statistically significant path coefficients between academic self-efficacy at Time 1 and achievement characteristics (test scores and school grades) at Time 2. In addition, analyses revealed small statistically significant path coefficients between achievement characteristics (test scores and school grades) and academic self-efficacy.

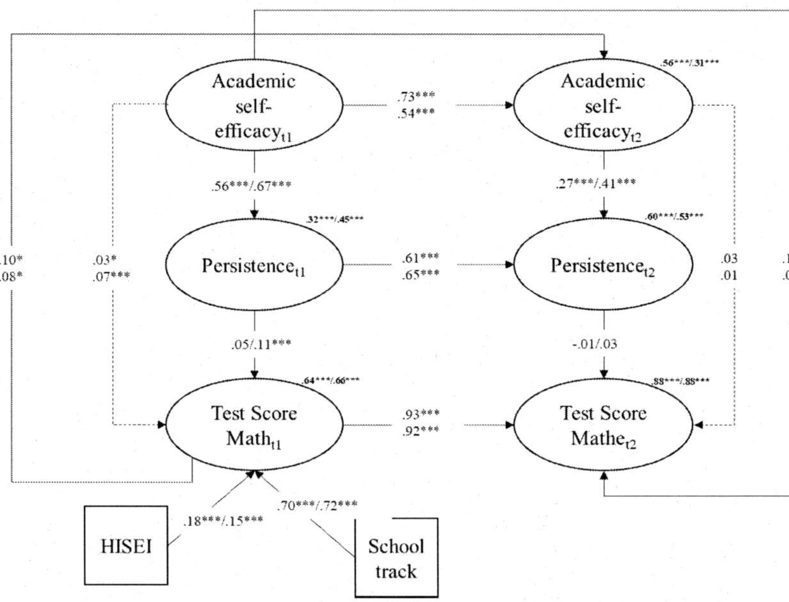

Note: First mentioned path coefficient female students‘, second mentioned path coefficient male students‘; t1 = measurement time point 1; t2 = measurement time point 2. *$p < .05$. **$p < .01$. ***$p < .001$.

Figure 5. Multi-group structural mediation model of academic self-efficacy via persistence on math test scores over time among female and male students.

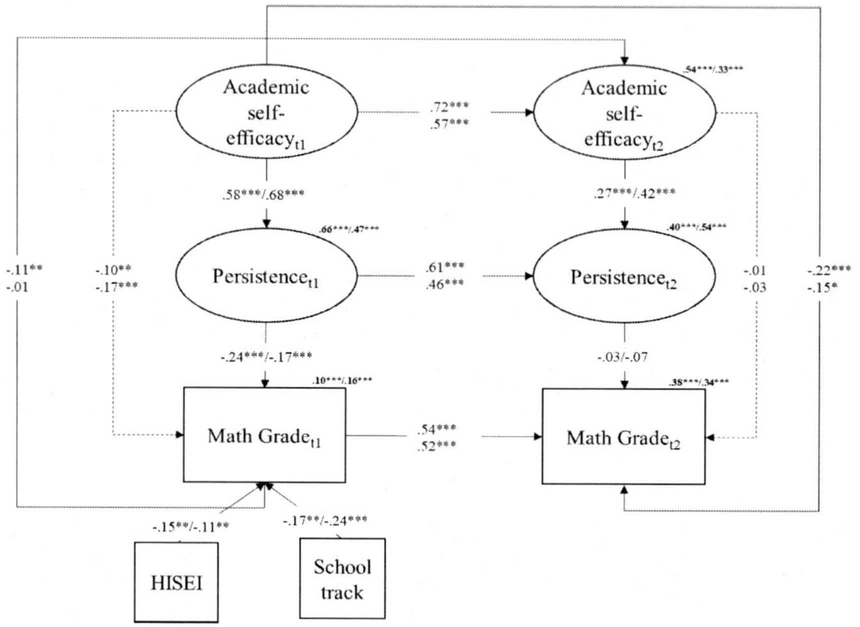

Note: First mentioned path coefficient female students', second mentioned path coefficient male students'; t1 = measurement time point 1; t2 = measurement time point 2. *$p < .05$. **$p < .01$. ***$p < .001$.

Figure 6. Multi-group structural mediation model of academic self-efficacy via persistence on math grades over time among female and male students.

Gender Differences

To examine gender differences in the relationships between academic self-efficacy, persistence, and achievement characteristics (test scores and school grades), we estimated multigroup structural equation models (see Figure 5 [test scores model] and Figure 6 [school grades model] as well as Table 5 for model fit criteria). Compared to the overall model (Figures 3 [test scores model] and 4 [math grades] as well as Table 5 for model fit criteria), the gender-specific model revealed differential path coefficients from academic self-efficacy via persistence to math test scores. There were statistically significant gender differences in path coefficients for the relation between persistence and math test scores, indicating that boys, but not girls, seemed to benefit from persistence when solving math problems in standardized tests (*W*

= 2.12, *df* = 1, *p* < .10; see Figure 5). However, girls' academic self-efficacy seemed to benefit more from their prior math grades than boys (*W* = 2.41, *df* = 1, *p* < .10; see Figure 6).

Differences between Students from Immigrant and Non-Immigrant Backgrounds

Largely constant coefficients explained the differences in math performance between subgroups of students from immigrant and non-immigrant backgrounds (see Figures 7 and 8; and Table 5 for model fit criteria) in comparison to the overall model (see Figures 3 and 4; and Table 5 for model fit criteria).

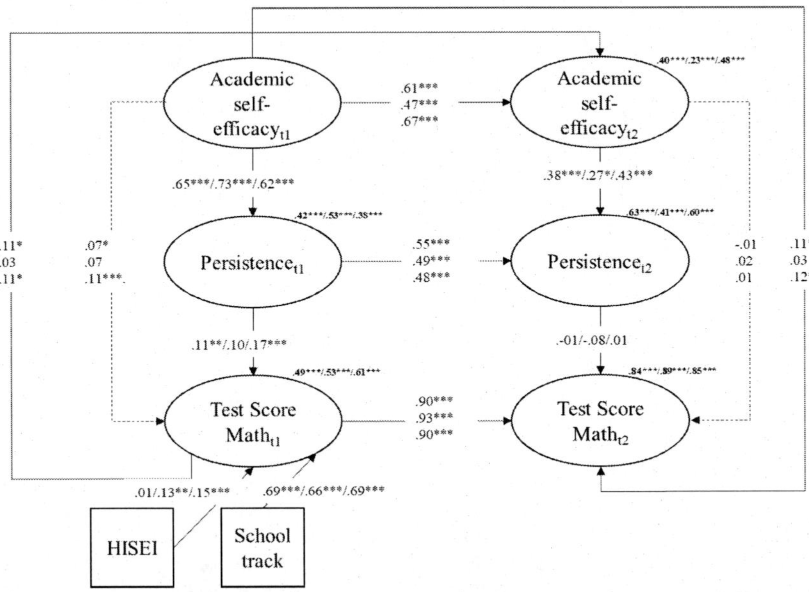

Note: First mentioned path coefficient students' with Turkish heritage, second mentioned path coefficient students' from former USSR states, third mentioned students' with no migrant background; t1 = measurement time point 1; t2 = measurement time point 2. *$p < .05$. **$p < .01$. ***$p < .001$.

Figure 7. Multi-group structural mediation model of academic self-efficacy via persistence on math test scores over time among students from immigrant and non-immigrant backgrounds.

There were statistically significant differences in the path coefficients explaining math achievement measured via standardized tests for students with origins in the former USSR compared to students from non-immigrant backgrounds. These showed that prior test scores were not relevant for later academic self-efficacy ($W = 2.09$, $df = 1$, $p < .10$; see Figure 7) and prior academic self-efficacy not relevant for later test scores ($W = 2.87$, $df = 1$, $p < .10$; see Figure 7). For school grades, there was only one significant difference in the path coefficient to later academic self-efficacy for Turkish-origin students compared to students from non-immigrant backgrounds ($W = 1.67$, $df = 1$, $p < .10$; see Figure 8).

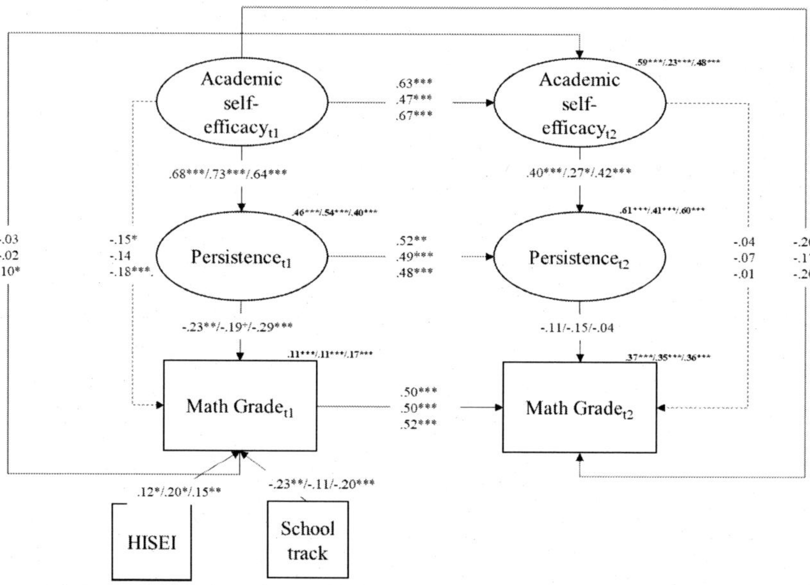

Note: First mentioned path coefficient students‘ with Turkish heritage, second mentioned path coefficient students‘ from former USSR states, third mentioned students‘ with no migrant background; t1 = measurement time point 1; t2 = measurement time point 2. *$p < .05$. **$p < .01$. ***$p < .001$.

Figure 8. Multi-group structural mediation model of academic self-efficacy via persistence on math grades over time among students from immigrant and non-immigrant backgrounds.

Discussion

This article aimed to investigate the significance of academic self-efficacy mediated via persistence for elements of math achievement not only over two time points but also as measured by standardized test scores versus school grades. It examined whether the self-enhancement position, which recent research has identified as characterizing the relationship between academic self-efficacy and achievement characteristics (Schöber et al., 2018), also holds for school grades reported back to students. It also investigated gender differences and differences by immigrant background by comparing the individual path coefficients between subgroups.

Mediation via Persistence

We examined core assumptions about the relationship between self-related beliefs, achievement self-enhancement, and reciprocal effect models (Calsyn and Kenny, 1977), and we compared girls versus boys and subgroups of students from immigrant versus non-immigrant backgrounds. The few existing results on the relationship between academic self-efficacy and math achievement in terms of test scores and school grades favor the self-enhancement position. On the one hand, this ma be because the relationship between academic self-efficacy and math achievement is mediated completely via persistence. On the other hand, it is because correlations between academic self-efficacy and math performance over time are statistically significant suggesting a reciprocal relationship. These results are consistent with Galla et al.'s (2014) findings, although they examined persistence as estimated by teachers as a mediator of the relationship between academic self-efficacy and achievement characteristics (Galla et al., 2014). These results also support Bandura's (1997) assumptions that only a perceived and successful self-enhancement can lead to the development of self-efficacy.

Group-Specific Differences

In the group-specific comparisons, the self-enhancement position was found to explain the relationship between math performance measured by standardized tests and self-efficacy only for boys. However, relationships between academic self-efficacy and math grades can be assumed for both girls and boys according to the self-enhancement position. Girls also benefit from persistence in terms of their math grades but not their performance on standardized tests. This suggests that girls' effectiveness beliefs are not significant for their actual math performance, but are important for the grading of math classroom performance, which, according to previous empirical studies, incorporates additional information beyond math test performance (Lubienski, Robinson, Crane, and Ganley, 2013). Furthermore, only girls' math test scores seem to profit from positive developments in general school-related effectiveness beliefs. It seems to be a non-subject-specific perception of success that girls experience in the male-connoted subject of math that leads to the development of academic self-efficacy (Pajares and Valiante, 2001).

The subgroup-specific analyses based on region of origin assessed the assumption that students whose families come from more collectivist societies will benefit less in terms of their academic self-efficacy from individual experiences of success. This could be confirmed only for students with origins in the former USSR. These results support the theoretical assumptions that the perception and evaluation of the self is differential and depends on sociocultural determinants (Kagitcibasi, 1997; Tafarodi and Walters, 1999). This is consistent with findings from other studies. It seems that other variables, such as feedback and support—especially from the family—are of greater importance for developing self-efficacy than the perception and evaluation of one's own successes (Di Giunta et al., 2010; Earley, Gibson, and Chen, 1999; Klassen, 2004).

Limitations and Implications for Future Research

The present study has certain limitations concerning the sample and the number and spacing of measurement occasions. The sample includes only 7th-grade students from four German states. Replicating the analyses in other grades and other regions could help to contextualize the results. The number of measurement occasions and the interval between them can be considered rather small for drawing inferences about a possible reciprocal relationship. Studies with a higher number of measurement occasions over a longer period could confirm the reciprocal effects (Caprara et al., 2001). Moreover, the results do not allow any conclusions on which other variables are significant for the development of academic self-efficacy among students with origins in the former USSR, perhaps experiences of support within the family. Furthermore, the results provide no explanations as to why the anticipated relationships were not found for Turkish-origin students, despite a number of studies describing Turkey as a rather collectivist society (Minkov et al., 2017).

Conclusion

In conclusion, this paper was able to confirm for this sample that the relationship between academic self-efficacy and math performance is mediated via persistence, thus testing and partially confirming Bandura's (1997) theoretical postulate. Group-specific analyses indicated that these constructs can indeed be compared across subgroups due to measurement invariance, but function differentially between them. This is not due to the functionality of the self-efficacy construct itself, but rather to stereotypes or differential perceptions of the *self* and the evaluation of experiences of success in different sociocultural reference contexts.

References

Adams, Raymond, J., Margaret L. Wu, and Mark Wilson. 2012. "ACER ConQuest 3.0.1. "*Camberwell: Australian Council for Educational Research.*

Bandura, Albert. 1997. *Self-efficacy: The exercise of control.* New York, NY: W. H. Freeman.

Bassi, Marta, Steca, Patrizia, Delle Fave, Antonella, and Caprara, Gian Vittorio. 2007. "Academic self-efficacy beliefs and quality of experience in learning." *Journal of Youth and Adolescence* 36, no. 3:301-312.

Beller, Michal, and Gafni, Naomi. 2000. "Can item format (multiple choice vs. open-ended) account for gender differences in mathematics achievement?" *Sex roles* 42, no. 1-2:1-21.

Bonneville-Roussy, Arielle, Vallerand, Robert J., and Bouffard, Thérèse. 2013. "The roles of autonomy support and harmonious and obsessive passions in educational persistence." *Learning and Individual Differences* 24:22-31.

Brandstätter, Veronika. 2014. Persistenz. In *Dorsch – Lexikon der Psychologie, 18. Auflage,* edited by Markus A. Wirtz, 1165. Bern: Hogrefe Verlag.

Britner, Shari L., and Pajares, Frank. 2001. "Self-efficacy beliefs, motivation, race, and gender in middle school science." *Journal of women and Minorities in Science and Engineering* 7, no. 4:271-285.

Brown, Timothy A. 2006. *Confirmatory factor analysis for applied research.* New York: Guilford.

Calsyn, Robert J., and David A. Kenny. 1977. "Self-concept of ability and perceived evaluation of others: Cause or effect of academic achievement?." *Journal of Educational Psychology* 69, no. 2:136-145.

Caprara, Gian Vittorio, Michele Vecchione, Guido Alessandri, Maria Gerbino, and Claudio Barbaranelli. 2011. "The contribution of personality traits and self-efficacy beliefs to academic achievement: A longitudinal study." *British Journal of Educational Psychology* 81, no. 1:78-96.

Chin, Dorothy, and Velma A. Kameoka. 2002. "Psychosocial and contextual predictors of educational and occupational self-efficacy among Hispanic inner-city adolescents." *Hispanic Journal of Behavioral Sciences* 24, no. 4:448-464.

Dickhäuser, Oliver, Marc-Andre Reinhard, and Chris Englert. 2011. "Of course I will...": The combined effect of certainty and level of expectancies on persistence and performance." *Social Psychology of Education* 14, no. 4:519-528.

Di Giunta, Laura, Nancy Eisenberg, Anne Kupfer, Patrizia Steca, Carlo Tramontano, and Gian Vittorio Caprara. 2010. "Assessing perceived empathic and social self-efficacy across countries." *European Journal of Psychological Assessment* 26, no. 2:77-86.

Docan, Tony N. 2006. "Positive and negative incentives in the classroom: An analysis of grading systems and student motivation." *Journal of Scholarship of Teaching and Learning* 6, no. 2:21-40.

Duckworth, Angela. 2016. *Grit: The power of passion and perseverance.* New York, NY: Scribner.

Duckworth, Angela Lee, and Martin E. P. Seligman. 2006. "Self-discipline gives girls the edge: Gender in self-discipline, grades, and achievement test scores." *Journal of Educational Psychology* 98, no. 2:198.

Dweck, Carol S. 2002. The development of ability conceptions, In *Development of Achievement Motivation*, edited by Allan Wigfield, and Jacquelynne S. Eccles, 57–88. San Diego, CA: Academic Press.

Earley, P. Christopher, Christina B. Gibson, and Chao C. Chen. 1999. "How did I do?" versus "How did we do?" Cultural contrasts of performance feedback use and self-efficacy." *Journal of Cross-Cultural Psychology* 30, no. 5:594-619.

Enders, Craig K. 2010. *Applied missing data analysis.* New York: Guilford.

Faber, Günter, and Elfriede Billmann-Mahecha. 2010. "Praxis der Notengebung–Probleme, Erfordernisse und Möglichkeiten aus pädagogisch-psychologischer Sicht [The practice of giving school grades: Problems, requirements, and opportunities form the perspective of educational psychology]." *Lernchancen* 13, no. 74:30–33.

Galla, Brian M., Jeffrey J. Wood, Eli Tsukayama, Kim Har, Angela W. Chiu, and David A. Langer. 2014. "A longitudinal multilevel model analysis of the within-person and between-person effect of effortful engagement and academic self-efficacy on academic performance." *Journal of School Psychology* 52, no. 3:295-308.

Ganzeboom, Harry B. G., Paul M. de Graaf, Donald J. Treiman, and Jan de Leeuw. 1992. *A standard international socioeconomic index of occupational status* (WORC Reprint). Tilburg: WORC, Work and Organization Research Centre.

Gebhardt, Markus, Dominique Patrizia Rauch, Julia Mang, Christine Sälzer, and Petra Stanat. 2013. "Mathematische Kompetenz von Schülerinnen und Schülern mit Zuwanderungshintergrund [Math competences of students from immigrant backgrounds]" In *PISA 2012. Fortschritte und Herausforderungen in Deutschland,* edited by Manfred Prenzel, Christine Sälzer, Eckhard Klieme, and Olaf Köller, 275–308. Münster: Waxmann.

Goldhammer, Frank, Johannes Naumann, Annette Stelter, Krisztina Tóth, Heiko Rölke, and Eckhard Klieme. 2014. "The Time on Task Effect in Reading and Problem Solving Is Moderated by Task Difficulty and Skill: Insights from a Computer-Based Large-Scale Assessment." *Journal of Educational Psychology* 106:608–626.

Grigg, Sara, Harsha N. Perera, Peter McIlveen, and Zvetomira Svetleff. 2018. "Relations among math self-efficacy, interest, intentions, and achievement: A social cognitive perspective." *Contemporary Educational Psychology* 53:73–86.

Grob, Urs, and Katharina Maag Merki. 2001. *Überfachliche Kompetenzen. Theoretische Grundlegung und empirische Erprobung eines Indikatorensystems* [General competencies: Theoretical basis and empirical testing of a system of indicators]. Bern, Switzerland: Peter Lang.

Hayes, Andrew F., and Kristopher J. Preacher. 2010. "Quantifying and testing indirect effects in simple mediation models when the constituent paths are nonlinear." *Multivariate Behavioral Research* 45, no. 4:627-660.

Hofstede, Geert. 2001. *Culture's consequences: Comparing values, behaviors, institutions and organizations across nations*. Thousand Oaks, CA: Sage.

Höhne, Elisabeth, and Lysann Zander. 2019. "Sources of male and female students' belonging uncertainty in the computer sciences." *Frontiers in psychology* 10:1740.

Houtte, Mieke Van. 2004. "Gender context of the school and study culture, or how the presence of girls affects the achievement of boys." *Educational Studies* 30, no. 4:409-423.

Hu, Li-tze, and Peter M. Bentler. 1999. "Cutoff criteria for fit indexes in covariance structure analysis: Conventional criteria versus new alternatives." *Structural Equation Modeling: a Multidisciplinary Journal* 6, no. 1:1-55.

Huang, Chiungjung. 2013. "Gender differences in academic self-efficacy: a meta-analysis." *European Journal of Psychology of Education* 28, no. 1:1–35.

Husain, Muna, and Daniel Millimet. 2009. "The mythical 'boy crisis'?" *Economics of Education Review* 28, no. 1:38–48.

Hwang, Mae Hyang, Hee Cheol Choi, Anna Lee, Jennifer D. Culver, and Brian Hutchison. 2016. "The relationship between self-efficacy and academic achievement: A 5-year panel analysis." *The Asia-Pacific Education Researcher* 25, no. 1:89–98.

Jerusalem, Matthias, and Lars Satow. 1999. "Schulbezogene Selbstwirksamkeitserwartung [School-related self-efficacy expectation]." In *Skalen zur Erfassung von Lehrerund Schülermerkmalen. Dokumentation der psychometrischen Verfahren im Rahmen der wissenschaftlichen Begleitung des Modellversuchs Selbstwirksame Schulen,* edited by Ralf Schwarzer, and Matthias Jerusalem, 15–16. Berlin, Germany: R. Schwarzer.

Kagitcibasi, Cigdem. 1997. "Individualism and collectivism." In *Handbook of cross-cultural psychology: Social behavior and applications,* edited by John W. Berry, Marshall H. Segall, and Cigdem Kagitçibasi, 1–49. Boston, MA: Allyn & Bacon.

Klassen, Robert M. 2004. "Optimism and realism: A review of self-efficacy from a cross-cultural perspective." *International Journal of Psychology*, 39 no. 3:205–230.

Kunter, Mareike, Gundel Schümer, Cordula Artelt, Jürgen Baumert, Eckhard Klieme, Michael Neubrand, Manfred Prenzel, Ulrich Schiefele, Wolfgang Schneider, Petra Stanat, Klaus-Jürgen Tillmann, Manfred Weiß. 2002. *PISA 2000: Dokumentation der Erhebungsinstrumente*. Berlin, Germany: Max Planck Institute for Human Development.

Lehmann, Rainer H., Rüdiger Gänsfuß, and Rainer Peek. 1999. *Aspekte der Lernausgangslage und der Lernentwicklung von Schülerinnen und Schülern an Hamburger Schulen — Klassenstufe 7* [Aspects of learning capabilities and learning developments of students at Hamburg schools: Grade 7]. Hamburg, Germany: Landesinstitut für Lehrerbildung und Schulentwicklung.

Liem, Arief Darmanegara, Shun Lau, and Youyan Nie. 2008. "The role of self-efficacy, task value, and achievement goals in predicting learning strategies, task disengagement, peer relationship, and achievement outcome." *Contemporary Educational Psychology* 33, no. 4:486–512.

Little, Roderick J. A. 1988. "A test of missing completely at random for multivariate data with missing values." *Journal of the American statistical Association* 83, no. 404:1198-1202.

Lubienski, Sarah T., Joseph P. Robinson, Corinna C. Crane, and Colleen M. Ganley. 2013. "Girls' and boys' mathematics achievement, affect, and experiences: Findings from ECLS-K." *Journal for Research in Mathematics Education* 44, no. 4:634–645.

Malmberg, Lars- Erik, and Andrew J. Martin. 2019. "Processes of students' effort exertion, competence beliefs and motivation: Cyclic and dynamic effects of learning experiences within school days and school subjects." *Contemporary Educational Psychology* 58:299–309.

Marsh, Herbert W. 1990. "The structure of academic self-concept: The Marsh/Shavelson model." *Journal of Educational psychology* 82, no. 4:623-636.

McFarlin, Dean B., Roy F. Baumeister, and Jim Blascovich. 1984. "On knowing when to quit: Task failure, self-esteem, advice, and nonproductive persistence." *Journal of Personality* 52, no. 2:138–155.

McIntyre, Nora A., M. Tim Mainhard, and Robert M. Klassen. 2017. "Are you looking to teach? Cultural, temporal and dynamic insights into expert teacher gaze." *Learning and Instruction* 49:41–53.

Mittag, Waldemar, Dietmar Kleine, and Matthias Jerusalem. 2002. "Evaluation der schulbezogenen Selbstwirksamkeit von Sekundarschülern [Evaluation of school-related self-efficacy in secondary school students]." *Zeitschrift für Pädagogik Beiheft* 44:145–173.

Minkov, Michael, Pinaki Dutt, Michael Schachner, Oswaldo Morales, Carlos Sanchez, Janar Jandosova, Yerlan Khassenbekow, and Ben Mudd. 2017. "A revision of

Hofstede's individualism-collectivism dimension." *Cross Cultural & Strategic Management* 24, no. 3:386–404.

Muthén, Linda K., and Bengt O. Muthén. 1998–2012. *Mplus User's Guide*. Los Angeles, CA: Muthén & Muthén.

Neumann, Marko, Anne Milek, Kai Maaz, and Cornelia Gresch. 2010. "Zum Einfluss der Klassenzusammensetzung auf den Übergang von der Grundschule in die weiterführenden Schulen [How class composition influences the transition from elementary to secondary school]." In *Der Übergang von der Grundschule in die weiterführende Schule-Leistungsgerechtigkeit und regionale, soziale und ethnisch-kulturelle Disparitäten,* edited by Kai Maaz, Jürgen Baumert, Cornelia Gresch, and Nele McElvany, 229-252. Berlin, Germany: BMBF.

Pajares, Frank. 1996. "Self-efficacy beliefs in academic settings." *Review of Educational Research* 66, no. 4:543–578.

Pajares, Frank, and Ellen L. Usher. 2008. "Self-efficacy, motivation, and achievement in school from the perspective of reciprocal determinism." *Advances in Motivation and Achievement* 15:391–423.

Pajares, Frank, and Giovanni Valiante. 2001. "Gender differences in writing motivation and achievement of middle school students: A function of gender orientation?" *Contemporary Educational Psychology* 26, no. 3:366–381.

Parker, Philip David, Herbert W. Marsh, Joseph Ciarrochi, Sarah Marshall, and Adel Salah Abduljabbar. 2014. "Juxtaposing math self-efficacy and self-concept as predictors of long-term achievement outcomes." *Educational Psychology* 34, no. 1:29–48.

Pintrich, Paul R. 2003. "A motivational science perspective on the role of student motivation in learning and teaching contexts." *Journal of Educational Psychology* 95, no. 4:667.

Ramírez-Rodríguez, R., and Dieter Dohmen. 2010. "Ethnisierung von geringer Bildung [Ethnicization of low education]." *Bildungsverlierer*, edited by Gudrun Quenzel, and Klaus Hurrelmann, 289–311. Wiesbaden, Germany: VS Verlag für Sozialwissenschaften.

Rost, Jürgen. 1996. *Lehrbuch Testtheorie, Testkonstruktion* [Textbook on test theory and test construction]. Vol. 2. Bern, Switzerland: Huber.

Rubin, Donald B. 1976. "Inference and missing data." *Biometrika* 63, no. 3:581–592.

Salili, Farideh, Chi-yue Chiu, and Simon Lai. 2001. "The influence of culture and context on students' motivational orientation and performance. In *Student motivation: The culture and context of learning,* edited by Salili Farideh, Chi-yue Chiu and Ying-yi Hong, 221-247. New York, NY: Kluwer.

Schöber, C., Schütte, K., Köller, O., McElvany, N., and Gebauer, M. M. (2018). Reciprocal effects between self-efficacy and achievement in mathematics and reading. *Learning and Individual Differences*, no. 63: 1-11.

Schunk, Dale H. 1995. "Self-efficacy, motivation, and performance." *Journal of Applied Sport Psychology* 7, no. 2:112–137.

Schunk, Dale H., and Ellen L. Usher. 2011. "Assessing self-efficacy for self-regulated learning." In *Educational psychology handbook series. Handbook of self-regulation of learning and performance,* edited by Barry J. Zimmermann, and Dale H. Schunk, 282–297. New York, NY: Routledge.

Sedikides, Constantine, and Aiden P. Gregg. 2008. "Self-enhancement: Food for thought." *Perspectives on Psychological Science* 3, no. 2:102-116.

Segeritz, Michael, Oliver Walter, and Petra Stanat. 2010. "Muster des schulischen Erfolgs von jugendlichen Migranten in Deutschland: Evidenz für segmentierte Assimilation [Academic success patterns of young migrants in Germany; Evidence of segmented assimilation]?" *Kölner Zeitschrift für Soziologie und Sozialpsychologie* 62, no. 1:113–138.

Skaalvik, Einar M., Roger A. Federici, and Robert M. Klassen. 2015. "Mathematics achievement and Self-efficacy. Relations with motivation for mathematics." *International Journal of Educational Research* 72:129–136.

Stoet, Gijsbert, and David C. Geary. 2013. "Sex differences in mathematics and reading achievement are inversely related: Within-and across-nation assessment of 10 years of PISA data." *PloS one* 8, no. 3: e57988. https://doi.org/10.1371/journal.pone.0057988.

Stride, Chris B., Gardner, S., Catley, N., and Thomas, F. 2015. "*Mpluscode for mediation, moderation, and moderated mediationmodels*." Accessed August, 2019. http://www.offbeat.group.shef.ac.uk/FIO/mplusmedmod.htm.

Tafarodi, Romin W. and Patricia Walters. 1999. "Individualism–collectivism, life events, and self-esteem: a test of two trade-offs." *European Journal of Social Psychology* 29, no. 5-6:797–814.

Talsma, Kate, Benjamin Schüz, Ralf Schwarzer, and Kimberley Norris. 2018. "I believe, therefore I achieve (and vice versa): A meta-analytic cross-lagged panel analysis of self-efficacy and academic performance." *Learning and Individual Differences* 61:136–150.

Vantieghem, Wendelien, Hans Vermeersch, and Mieke Van Houtte. 2014. "Transcending the gender dichotomy in educational gender gap research: The association between gender identity and academic self-efficacy." *Contemporary Educational Psychology* 39, no. 4:369–378.

Vollmeyer, Regina, and Falko Rheinberg. 2000. "Does motivation affect performance via persistence?" *Learning and Instruction* 10, no. 4:293–309.

Wang, Ming-Te, and Jacquelynne S. Eccles. 2013. "School context, achievement motivation, and academic engagement: A longitudinal study of school engagement using a multidimensional perspective." *Learning and Instruction* 28: 12-23.

Wang, Pei, Pei Zhou, Cheng-Hao Tan, and Peng-Cheng Zhang. 2017. "Effect of self-efficacy in stereotype activation." *Social Behavior and Personality: an international journal* 45, no. 3:469-476.

Zhao, Xinshu, John G. Lynch, and Qimei Chen. 2010. "Reconsidering Baron and Kenny: Myths and truths about mediation analysis." *Journal of Consumer Research* 37, no. 2:197-206.

Zimmerman, Barry J. 2000. "Self-efficacy: An essential motive to learn." *Contemporary Educational Psychology* 25, no. 1:82-91.

Chapter 4

Self-Compassion and Parenting

Thanh Minh Nguyen[1], Hang Thi Thu Dinh[2] and Giang Nguyen Hoang Le[3]

[1]Department of Psychology, Hoa Sen University, Ho Chi Minh City, Vietnam
[2]Research Institute of Early Childhood Education, Graduate School of Humanities and Social Sciences, Hiroshima University, Hiroshima, Japan
[3]Faculty of Education, Brock University, St. Catharines, Ontario, Canada

Open Thoughts: Parenting's Joy and Stress

> Being a parent is dirty and scary and beautiful and hard and miraculous and exhausting and thankless and joyful and frustrating all at once. It's everything.
>
> *Jill Smokler*

Parenting is a divine journey, but it can also bring stress and even burnout, defined as a state of severe and chronic exhaustion related to one's parenting role (Mikolajczak & Roskam, 2019). People often expect that parenting will turn out to be a beautiful and wonderful experience (Feldman & Nash, 1984). The rewards of parenthood include increased meaning in life (Roy et al., 2013), subjective well-being (Kohler et al., 2005), and positive emotions (Nelson et al., 2013). However, there are grey areas of being parents that need to be further discussed. For example, Mikolajczak et al. (2019) indicate that stress in daily parenting may increase parental exhaustion. For parents, feeling burnout includes loss of joy during parenting, loss of time for self-care, loss of desire to stay connected physically and emotionally to the child (Mikolajczak et al., 2019). The transition to parenthood tends to be a time of chronic stress for most new parents, with a negative impact on relationship

In: The Importance of Self-Efficacy and Self-Compassion
Editor: James J. Carmona
ISBN: 978-1-68507-763-1

satisfaction, functioning, and increased depression toward parents (Cowan & Cowan, 2000; Karney & Bradbury, 2020; Mitnick et al., 2009; Evenson & Simon, 2005). The inconsistency in these research results shows us that parenthood is complex, and its effects on parents' mental and physical health are heterogeneous. Researchers have recently attempted to explain these mixed findings.

Mikolajczak and Roskam (2018) proposed a theoretical and clinical framework called the balance between Risks and Resources (BR2). According to the BR2 theory, protective factors for parents' mental health may include their characteristics (e.g., self-compassion), positive parenting styles (e.g., authoritative parenting), support from their spouses, and extended family (Mikolajczak & Roskam, 2018; Mikolajczak et al., 2019), etc. In contrast, risk factors include poor parenting styles (e.g., authoritarian, and harsh parenting), personal characteristics (e.g., perfectionism and self-judgment), lack of support from the partners and families, and their children's characteristics (e.g., children with special needs) (Mikolajczak & Roskam, 2018; Mikolajczak et al., 2019), etc. As a result, parental burnout syndrome occurs when parental protective and resource factors often fail to compensate for the demands and risks of parenting (Mikolajczak & Roskam, 2018). Hence, it is essential to improve parents' mental health and family functioning by providing resources that act as barriers to protecting parents and their children. Self-compassion is an influential protective factor in reducing stress for parents when they feel overwhelmed (Smallen et al., 2021) burnout (Mikolajczak & Roskam, 2019). Self-compassion serves as a shield preventing parents from stress and exhaustion on their parenting journey (Sirois et al., 2018).

In this chapter, firstly, we synthesize and examine research evidence on the relationship between parental self-compassion and parents' mental health. Secondly, we look into the role of parental self-compassion in parenting practices, such as reducing harmful parenting approaches while promoting positive parenting practices to strengthen the parent-child relationship. Thirdly, we investigate the direct and indirect effect of parents' self-compassion on children's outcomes (e.g., reducing problem behaviors and increasing quality of life). To conclude this chapter, we propose some suggestions for future research and practice to apply self-compassion to improve the quality of parenting.

Unpacking Self-Compassion

Inspired by Buddhist psychology, Neff (2003a, b) coined self-compassion as a way to accept the fact that we are imperfect. It is against the common sense that "being average is unacceptable" (Neff, 2011, p. 1) and that we are often pressured to be special and above average to feel deserved for what we have earned in an insanely competitive society. Self-compassion refers to an ability to understand contemplatively and mindfully the self when "suffering occurs through no fault of one's own" (Neff, 2011, p .4) and especially when life with many challenges is hard to encounter. Self-compassion is a reminder for people to learn about suffering that originates from their mistakes, failures, and inadequacies (Nguyen & Le, 2021).

Key to self-compassion, therefore, is a critical understanding of suffering, which is rooted in engaged Buddhism. Thich Nhat Hanh, the world's spiritual leader and a Zen Master, initiated and developed the term, engaged Buddhism, which is a Buddhist social movement seeking ways to cultivate the Buddhist ethics from meditation practice to help people delve into social, environmental, and personal suffering and injustice. It is immensely about changing one's mind, body, soul, and heart, to transform shame and guilt into self-acceptance (Khong & Nhat, 2014; Nhat, 2018). This is a practice of loving kindness. Through the mind of loving kindness, people learn that being alive is being able to feel hurt and embrace pains. It is essential to recognize that suffering is pivotal to feel alive, and understanding personal as well as others' suffering is key to self-forgiveness (Le et al., 2020; Nhat, 2018).

Inheriting from engaged Buddhism's notion of suffering and self-forgiveness, according to Neff (2003b), there are three foundational components of self-compassion: self-kindness, feelings of common humanity, and mindfulness. They overlap and mutually interact with one another. Self-kindness comes along with self-judgment, feelings of common humanity versus isolation, and mindfulness versus over-identification (Neff, 2011). First, self-kindness implies the tendency to show care and an understanding about ourselves over being extremely self-judgmental. Second, feelings of common humanity are central to self-compassion involving an ability to realize that people can fail, make mistakes, and feel inadequate in many ways (Neff, 2011). Nguyen and Le (2021) note that this second component stresses the fact that humans are flawed so possibilities for having errors in life are inevitable. Third, mindfulness illustrates a consciousness of the present moment "in a contemplative manner, and thus we with mindfulness will be able to critically ruminate on undesired aspects of ourselves and our lives" (Nguyen & Le, 2021, p. 2). Central to self-compassion is the capability to become enlightened that everyone can suffer and suffering is essential as a medium to extend compassion towards the self. Conceiving that fact mindfully, people will be able to have mental balance while they are facing stressful circumstances in their lives. Mindfulness becomes key to promoting self-compassion, and hence self-compassion is the most potential mechanism through which mindfulness can be linked to one's well-being (Hollis-Walker & Colosimo, 2011).

Self-Compassion and Parents' Mental Health

Despite differences in context, culture, and country within the parenting discourse, the study on parental mental health investigated that parental mental health was related to their parenting and children's long-term mental health outcomes (Reupert et al., 2013). Recent studies show that parents' self-compassion is a protective factor tightly associated with parental mental health (e.g., Jefferson et al., 2020; Sirois et al., 2018). In this regard, this section explores their relationship under the state of parental mental health.

Self-compassion was positively correlated with parent's mental health by boosting their well-being. Parents' well-being emanates from their happiness, work productivity, positive feelings about themselves and their children, and joy (Torbin et al., 2019; Bohadana et al., 2019). Literature on parents' mental health demonstrates self-compassion as a helpful and practical solution for enhancing parental mental health and well-being (e.g., Felder et al., 2016; Fonseca & Canavarro, 2017; Gouveia et al., 2016, Sirois et al., 2018). It enhances parental well-being by accepting the failures on their parenting, being non-judgmental when to be a perfect parent, and satisfying the children's needs (e.g., Geurtzen et al., 2014; Sirois et al., 2018). The high level of self-compassion can lead to the well-being of mental health.

The opposite of the well-being state is the mental health problems or mental illness referring to all mental disorders that can be diagnosed and feature abnormalities in cognition, emotion or mood, and the highest integrative aspects of human behavior, such as social interactions (U.S. Department of Health and Human Services, 2001). Parents become vulnerable to mental health problems due to the lack of parenting, especially the parent who was setting this role for the first time, the imbalance between the expectation and the real, and the resonance with other roles lead the people to fall in sustaining their mental health. Ruud et al. (2019) posit that up to 36% of patients seeking psychiatric treatment are parents caring for dependent children. This finding echoes the concern and essential support for the parent facing mental health problems.

Mental health problems are dangerous, leading to the low quality of parenting and children's outcomes. Parent's mental health problems were found as a harmful factor that negatively impacts their parenting abilities, identity, and parenting practices (Foster et al., 2011) by increasing stress and anxiety (Henderson et al., 2017), and putting parents at risk of socio-economic disadvantage, unemployment, marital conflict, and adverse effects on their children's development. Mental health problems also cause negative parenting behaviors, lack of attention to children's needs, increased dysfunction within the home (Wilson & Durbin, 2010), children's worse mental health, more behavioral problems during their youth (Schepman et al., 2011; Meadows et al., 2007), and have more significant distress than their non-exposed counterparts throughout adulthood (Kamis, 2020). The negativity of mental health problems in parenting needs to be addressed by a protective factor as parental self-compassion. Self-compassion helps prevent, reduce and heal mental health problems. It can reduce their strain, stress, anxiety, depression, and burnout (e.g., Felder et al., 2016; Fonseca & Canavarro, 2017; Gouveia et al., 2016, Sirois et al., 2018). It has negatively correlated with psychological distress parenting stress and increased their quality of parenting practices (Torbin et al., 2019; Bohadana et al., 2019).

Self-compassion, mindfulness, and concrete rumination were demonstrated to reduce parental burnout. Concrete ruminations are considered to be helpful to cope with difficulties. Both self-compassion and mindfulness were investigated as influential protection factors against parental burnout (Mikolajczak et al., 2018; Anclair et al., 2018). Self-compassion helps prevent parental burnout by reducing anxiety, depression symptoms (van Dam et al., 2011), and self-criticism (Sorkkila et al., 2020). Mindfulness can avert parental burnout by paying attention to the experience of the present moment and developing a non-judgmental (Kabat-Zinn, 2003; Neft & Germer, 2012). Both of those positive interventions are effective at improving parental depression, anxiety, stress, parents general health (e.g., Alexander, 2018; Taylor et al., 2016), enhancing parent-child positive interactions, and also reducing aggressive behavior and behavioral problems when working with their children (Neece, 2014).

In addition, self-compassion reduces parents' feelings of guilt and shame that are negative experiences in parenting (e.g., Liss & Erchull, 2015; Sirois et al., 2018). Although those emotions can help parents correct their future behavior in the nurture and educate their children (Tangney & Tracy, 2012), however, when they fail to control the feeling of shame and guilt, these emotions can be harmful to their well-being (Rangganadhan & Todorov, 2010). Negative emotions lead to other hostile states, i.e., depression (Foster et al., 2011). Sirois et al. (2018) and Johnson & O'Brien (2013) confirm that parents who have a higher level of self-compassion could reduce feelings of guilt and shame. Self-compassion is protective for feelings of guilt in the context of challenging parenting events by emphasizing self-kind rather than self-critical evaluations of oneself (Neff, 2003).

It was reported that one of the stress-alleviating factors that help decrease parental stress is parental self-compassion (Mikolajczak et al., 2018). Parenting stress has been defined as the stress that arises when the parenting demands exceed the parent's personal and social resources (e.g., parenting skills and knowledge, social support) to cope with those demands (Deater-Deckard, 2004). Parents may know how to implement recommended behavioral strategies, but they still find it difficult in handling stress. The situation becomes more challenging with more stress when parents face unexpected child behaviors (Hastings, 2002). Increasing parental self-compassion may be an effective intervention to improve parenting quality. Self-compassion also can boost other protective factors such as emotional intelligence, good child-rearing practices, time for leisure, and positive co-parenting (e.g., Felder et al., 2016; Psychogiou et al., 2016). As a result, mindfulness has been found to enable a more constructive response to parenting stress (Bogels et al., 2014). Self-compassion and mindfulness will improve marital functioning and the process of co-parenting (Bogels et al., 2010).

Self-Compassion and Parenting Practices

Parenting practices are considered essential factors that directly affect children's development (Bronfenbrenner & Moris, 2007). The constant interaction and support from parents to their children have helped increase positive psychological qualities in children while also helping to improve students' classroom peer status (Nguyen et al., 2020) and their academic achievement (Castro et al., 2015). In contrast, negative parenting styles such as neglect, authoritarian, and psychological control have increased their children's problems such as smartphone addiction (Kwak et al., 2018), social anxiety (Gulley et al., 2014), aggressive and somatic problems (Fuentes et al., 2014), while contributing to decreased academic achievement (Barber & Harmon, 2002). Parenting practices has become an essential conceptual framework in child and family research and has attracted significant interest from academics (Collins et al., 2000). The appeal of researchers has been evenly dispersed in addressing both the question of the effects of parenting style on children's development and their search for factors that may help increase positive parenting practices in the family context (Collins et al., 2000). It also delves into uncovering the contribution of positive psychological factors or, in other words, the source of parents' inner strength on their parenting journey (Kyriazos & Stalikas, 2018). As a result, self-compassion has become a concept of interest to researchers, and the findings from the previous studies also supported the hypothesis that self-compassion brought benefits to parenting practices (Nguyen et al., 2021; Gouveia et al., 2016; Lathren et al., 2021).

First of all, self-compassion contributes to the increase of positive parenting styles and a reduction of harmful parenting practices (Lathren et al., 2021; Nguyen et al., 2021). Recent studies have shown that self-compassion has increased mindful parenting (Moreira et al., 2015; Gouveia et al., 2016; Nguyen et al., 2021). Self-compassion helps parents (i) become aware of their emotional integrity, including positive and negative emotions, rather than ignore them, and (ii) recognize and respect their children's feelings and thoughts (Moreira et al., 2015). As a result, these characteristics enable parents to best regulate themselves in their daily interactions with their children. Self-compassionate parents tend to give children their full attention, attentively listen to, and support their children instead of judging them hastily and negatively, which results in an enhancement in mindful parenting (Moreira et al., 2015; Gouveia et al., 2016; Nguyen et al., 2021).

Additionally, parents with high levels of self-compassion frequently used authoritative styles in parenting, and they also reported low levels of authoritarian and permissive parenting styles (Gouveia et al., 2016). Self-compassionate parents look at their children's behavioral difficulties in a more positive light (Lathren et al., 2021). They can accept both their children's good and misbehaviors and recognize that there is an opportunity to help them acquire new skills. Self-compassionate parents also see children's behavioral problems as transient and related to the environmental context rather than the child's inherent characteristics (Psychogiou et al., 2016). When their children present behavioral problems, self-compassionate parents also used a problem-focused approach rather than criticizing themselves and their children (Psychogiou et al., 2016). As a result, these characteristics will help prevent parents away from placing undue demands on their children, using harsh discipline, or neglecting their children (the signs of authoritarian and permissive parenting styles). Self-compassion can also make it easier for parents to adopt a child-centered approach that describes authoritative parenting (characterized by warmth, support, and high parental requirements) (Gouveia et al., 2016).

The influence of compassion is not limited in parenting practices but extends to the close relationships between parents and children (Lathren et al., 2021). In intimate relationships such as parent and child, studies have shown that self-compassion has several benefits such as (i) increasing adaptive response to challenging situations interpersonal relationships, (ii) helping to enhance the quality of relationships, (iii) creating a balance of concern for self and others, and (iv) improve perceived supportiveness of others (Lathren et al., 2021). A recent longitudinal study by Fernandes et al. (2021) found that parents' self-compassion was significantly correlated with mother-infant bonding. Self-compassionate mothers frequently employ a mindful parenting approach, which helps reduce parental stress and ultimately increases bonding between themselves and their children (Fernandes et al., 2021). Parents with higher levels of self-compassion show more sensitivity, responsiveness, and warmth toward their children (Psychogiou et al., 2016), thereby contributing to an increase or decrease in the quality of attachments they establish (Cree, 2010). In summary, self-compassion is linked to parenting benefits, including increasing positive parenting approaches, reducing harmful parenting practices, and strengthening the bonding between parents and their children.

Furthermore, the most recent studies on the relationship between self-compassion and parenting practices use self-report measures and cross-sectional designs (Lathren et al., 2021). These approaches limit further insight into the bidirectional relationships that may have occurred between parents' self-compassion and parenting practices over time. Thus, longitudinal studies will enable the researcher to explore the interplay (or not) between self-compassion and parenting practices. In addition, future research will also benefit from using various other techniques to measure parental self-compassion (Lathren et al., 2021). For example, qualitative inquiries that include both parents' and child's perspectives or art-based approaches will provide additional data on the unique ways parental compassion can influence parenting behaviors in dynamic contexts.

Also, cross-cultural studies examining how self-compassion interacts with parenting are less prevalent (Lathren et al., 2020). Previous studies have also supported that self-compassion has adapted to parenting outcomes across cultures (Gouveia et al., 2016; Sirois et al., 2019). Parent-child interviews or focus groups exploring how parents and children think about self-compassion in different cultural groups will add to the theoretical understanding of the interaction between self-compassion and parenting practices in families with different backgrounds (Lathren et al., 2020). The mechanism of the relationship between parents' self-compassion and parenting practices is through both direct and indirect pathways (Nguyen et al., 2020; Psychogiou et al., 2016). However, studies that examine the moderators in the path from self-compassion to parenting practices are still very limited in the literature of this field. Several variables can influence an individual's self-compassion manifests, such as ethnicity/race, gender, age, childhood attachment profile (Murn & Steele, 2019; Pepping et al., 2014; Yarnell et al., 2015). Besides, it is likely that children's characteristics, such as behavior problems, mental health status, temperaments, etc., will also moderate the relationship between parents' self-compassion and parenting practices.

Self-Compassion and Children's Outcomes

> "Parents are the single greatest influence on children. The key to closing the gap in child outcomes is closing the gap in what families do with their children."
>
> *(Professor, Ariel Kalil – Director of the Center for Human Potential and Public Policy and Co-Director of the Behavioral Insights and Parenting Lab at the University of Chicago, Andrea, 2018)*

There is a body of literature of the influence of parents on children's outcomes in terms of their parenting (e.g., Maccoby, 2000; Wolicki et al., 2021; Shewark et al., 2021). Many studies indicate that self-compassion plays a crucial role in building a positive parent-child relationship associated with children's outcomes, behavior, internalizing and externalizing problems, and mental health (e.g., Moreira et al., 2015; Neff & Faso, 2015; Psychogiou et al., 2016).

Self-compassion has been well-researched in reducing preschool children's externalizing symptoms (Townshend et al., 2016), child-directed criticism (Psychogiou et al., 2016), children behavior problems (Beer et al., 2013), as well as can improve children well-being and mental health (e.g., Beer et al., 2013; Gouveia et al., 2016).

Parental self-compassion enhances children's well-being and decreases children's mental health problems. The low self-compassion that can lead to parenting stress is strongly associated with adverse psychological outcomes in children (e.g., Neece, 2014; Robinson & Neece, 2015) and directly impacts their children's psychological well-being (Osborne et al., 2008). Shewark et al. (2021) found that a child's mental health problems, including anger and sadness, were associated with more hostile parenting and were not associated with warm parenting. Those feelings were then linked to an increase in child behavioral problems. Due to this proportional relationship between the mental health of parents and children, to improve children's mental health, parents need to care for themselves to enhance self-compassion that helps improve their mental health.

The level of parental self-compassion has the different level of influence on children's behavior. The self-compassion of parents becomes the model of self-compassion for their children. The feeling of parents about their parenting roles and how parents relate to themselves in difficult or distressing situations have a relationship with their parent's attachment orientations and continue to affect their children (Moreira et al., 2015). Lathren et al. (2021) suggest that parents' self-compassion is linked to supportive parenting behavior that affects the relationship between parents and their children. The positive parent-child relationship created by mindfulness parenting can foster children's psychological functioning, behavior, and well-being (e.g., Duncan et al., 2009, 2015; Lippold et al., 2015). Also, children's behavior problems can be reduced by their self-compassion, which was shaped by their parents' self-compassion. By contrast, children's behavioral problems were increased when their parents were at low self-compassion. If parents cannot cope successfully with significant stressors and effectively manage mental health issues, the effectiveness of behavioral therapies may be restricted (Osborne et al., 2008), and children's behavioral problems may increase (Mcgrath, 2013; Neece et al., 2012).

The mindfulness of self-compassion also has a positively relationship on children's behavior. Mindfulness parents can develop a calm and consistent stance toward their children; they might also interrupt a judgmental attitude towards the child's behavior, enjoy in the present moment, and express more warmth and less negativity during interacting with their child (Duncan et al., 2009; Miller et al., 2015). Mindfulness parents increase satisfaction in their parenting skills and reduce external behavior problems, which results in improved social skills for their children, a reduction of the rigors of parenting, and the symptoms of anxiety and depression in adolescents (Singh et al., 2007; Duncan et al., 2015; Geurtzen et al., 2014).

In addition, children's behaviors are also associated with the parental involvement that is affected by their self-compassion. Parental involvement typically involves parents' behaviors at home and in schools to support their children's educational progress. It also characterizes parents' values and attitudes regarding education and their aspirations for their children (Ebere Adimora, 2019; Park & Holloway, 2016). Nokali et al. (2010) found that within-child improvements in parental involvement predict a decline in problem behaviors and an improvement in their behaviors in society. Children's behaviors reflect what they are feeling and reflect the environment, as well as the behaviors of others. Parents with self-compassion considers the cause of their children's behavior to external factors, is less critical, and uses fewer distressed reactions to cope with their children's emotions. They do not show judgment but empathy to children's behaviors, which will boost their good behavior and calm with their behavioral problems.

Children's outcomes are reflected explicitly through children's academic achievements that can be enhanced by parents' self-compassion through parental involvement and attachment. Several studies show that parental involvement in the education of children that was influenced by parental self-compassion is a key factor for improving children's academic outcomes (e.g., Lara & Saracostti, 2019; Tárraga et al., 2017). Parental involvement may not directly influence children's academic outcomes. It indirectly enhances academic achievement by promoting children's motivation and persistence in challenging educational tasks (el Nokali et al., 2010), improving children's self-esteem, academic performance (Garbacz et al., 2017), school retention, and attendance (Ross, 2016). Sheldon (2009) also shows that successful students have strong academic support from their involved parents. Parents promote children's educational achievement by providing a safe and healthy environment, appropriate learning experiences, support, and a positive attitude about school (ĐUrišić & Bunijevac, 2017).

Children's cognitive performance also is boosted by parent-child attachment. West et al. (2012) found that the more secured mother-child attachment is, the better school performance and higher IQs (Intelligence Quotient) in middle childhood are. The maternal attachment-related anxiety and avoidance toward their mothers can affect their children's quality of life scores through lower levels of mothers' self-compassion and higher levels of parenting stress (Moireira et al., 2015). The tightly connection with parents becomes the scaffolding, the ladder that children can feel safe, comfortable, and confidence to show off themselves at home, and at school.

Moreover, parental self-compassion can enhance the outcomes of children with special needs (e.g., Cachiaet al., 2016, Neece, 2014, Neff & Paso, 2015; Wong et al., 2016). Parents of children with special needs may face more unique challenges and negative experiences than parents of typically developing children (e.g., Hayes & Watson, 2013, Torber et al., 2019). These difficulties, for instance, the feeling that their children can be rejected by society, the budget problem, the demand for special education for their children, and children's behavioral problems, can lead them to parental stress and psychological distress that affect the quality of their parenting, and of course, will affect their children's development (e.g., Cachia et al., 2016, Keenan et al., 2016). Self-compassion helps reduce the stress for parents of young children with developmental delay was examined in reducing children's behavior problems (Neece, 2014, Cahia et al., 2016), particular autism spectrum disorder (ASD) symptoms (e.g., Beer et al., 2013, Jones et al., 2014), aggression, non-compliance, self-injury, and increasing their social behavior (Singh et al., 2007).

Final Thoughts: A New Journey Begins

There is a growing amount of work on self-compassion in relation to stress coping mechanism (Nguyen & Le, 2021), mental health (Voci et al., 2019), psychological well-being (Allen et al., 2012; Wood et al., 2009), nursing education and training (Hofmeyer et al., 2020), and even religious educational philosophy (Le et al., 2020). Self-compassion is theorized and studied as a positive disposition exhibited towards the self in times of trouble and failures (Neff, 2003). Self-compassion refers to mindfulness and self-acceptance which result in a deep understanding of suffering caused by trials and tribulations as inevitable components of our lives.

There are links between self-compassion and parents' mental health, especially parental burnout, which is pernicious feeling when parents find it difficult in navigating resources to deal with stress of parenting. Parental burnout can place parents at risk of psychological well-being issues, such as loss of hope, love, and self-care that always happen on their parenthood journey (Mikolajczak et al., 2019). In this chapter, we have delved into literature of the role of self-compassion in improving parents' well-being. It is well reported that self-compassion plays a protective role in parental mental health since self-compassion is a booster for parents' wellness emotionally and physically, including staying productive and positive in child-rearing. Integrating self-compassion into parenting helps them understand mindfully the meaning of being parents, which encompasses joy, love, exhaustion, and hopelessness at the same time. They are interwoven to uphold the divine role of parents in the development of a child.

Self-compassion is critical in enhancing parenting practices, such as mindful parenting (Moreira et al., 2015). Cultivating self-compassion in parenting makes parents better aware of their emotions, which means they feel essential in embracing various genres of their feelings as mindful parents. By doing so, they will be able to learn and honour their children's emotions and thoughts when they interact with one another. Mindfulness parents who have self-compassion are authoritative parents always viewing and treating their children's misbehaviours with calm, kindness, and patience. We are writing this chapter with an in-depth understanding of the significance of self-compassion in building mindful parenting style as it helps address critical mental health issues faced by modern parents, such as parental burnout. Although there are studies on self-compassion and parents of special needs children, we still call out for more critical research on the importance of self-compassion in enhancing the well-being of this special group of parents and especially in making difference in the development of children with difficulties. Moving from that advocacy for further research, specific mental health issues faced by these parents necessitate the needs for more parenting practices that are potentially self-compassion integrated.

References

Allen, A. B., Goldwasser, E. R., & Leary, M. R. (2012). Self-compassion and well-being among older adults. *Self and Identity,* 11(4), 428-453.

Anclair, M., Lappalainen, R., Muotka, J., & Hiltunen, A. J. (2017). Cognitive behavioural therapy and mindfulness for stress and burnout: a waiting list controlled pilot study comparing treatments for parents of children with chronic conditions. *Scandinavian Journal of Caring Sciences,* 32(1), 389– 396. https://doi.org/10.1111/scs.12473.

Andrea, P. C. (2018, August 6). Interview: Changing Parental Behavior with Behavioral Tools Can Help Children Reach Their Full Potential. *Early Childhood Development.* https://blogs.iadb.org/desarrollo-infantil/en/parental-behavior-influences-child-development/

Barber, B. K., & Harmon, E. L. (2002). Violating the self: Parental psychological control of children and adolescents. In B. K. Barber (Ed.), *Intrusive parenting: How psychological control affects children and adolescents* (pp. 15–52). American Psychological Association. https://doi.org/10.1037/10422002.

Bhugra, D., Till, A., & Sartorius, N. (2013). What is mental health? *International Journal of Social Psychiatry,* 59(1), 3–4. https://doi.org/10.1177/0020764012463315.

Birnie, K., Speca, M., & Carlson, L. E. (2010). Exploring self-compassion and empathy in the context of mindfulness-based stress reduction (MBSR). *Stress and Health,* 26(5), 359–371. https://doi.org/10.1002/smi.1305.

Borre, A., & Kliewer, W. (2014). Parental strain, mental health problems, and parenting practices: A longitudinal study. *Personality and Individual Differences,* 68, 93–97. https://doi.org/10.1016/j.paid.2014.04.014.

Bronfenbrenner, U., & Morris, P. A. (2006). *The Bioecological Model of Human Development.* John Wiley & Sons Inc.

Collins, W. A., Maccoby, E., Steinberg, L., Hetherington, E. M., & Bornstein, M. H. (2000). Contemporary research on parenting: The case for nature and nurture. *American Psychologist,* 55.

Cowan, C. P., & Cowan, P. A. (2000). *When partners become parents: The big life change in couples.* Lawrence Erlbaum.

Cree, M. (2010). Compassion-focused therapy with perinatal and mother-infant distress. *International Journal of Cognitive Therapy,* 3(2), 159–171. https://doi.org/10.1521/ijct.2010.3.2.159.

ĐUrišić, M., & Bunijevac, M. (2017). Parental Involvement as an Important Factor for Successful Education. *Center for Educational Policy Studies Journal,* 7(3), 137–153. https://doi.org/10.26529/cepsj.291.

Ebere Adimora, D., Neejide Onyishi, C., & Nonye Helen, U. (2019a). Parental Involvement as a Correlate of Academic Self-Efficacy of Secondary School Students. *International Journal of Secondary Education,* 7(3), 69. https://doi.org/10.11648/j.ijsedu.20190703.12.

Ebere Adimora, D., Neejide Onyishi, C., & Nonye Helen, U. (2019b). Parental Involvement as a Correlate of Academic Self-Efficacy of Secondary School Students. *International Journal of Secondary Education*, 7(3), 69. https://doi.org/10.11648/j.ijsedu.20190703.12.

El Nokali, N. E., Bachman, H. J., & Votruba-Drzal, E. (2010). Parent Involvement and Children's Academic and Social Development in Elementary School. *Child Development,* 81(3), 988–1005. https://doi.org/10.1111/j.1467-8624.2010.01447.x.

Evenson RJ, Simon RW. (2005). Clarifying the Relationship Between Parenthood and Depression. *Journal of Health and Social Behavior,* 46(4):341-358. doi:10.1177/002214650504600403.

Felder, J. N., Lemon, E., Shea, K., Kripke, K., & Dimidjian, S. (2016). Role of self-compassion in psychological well-being among perinatal women. *Archives of Women's Mental Health,* 19(4), 687– 690. https://doi.org/10.1007/s00737-016-0628-2.

Feldman, S. S., Nash, S. (1984). The transition from expectancy to parenthood: Impact of the firstborn child on men and women. *Sex Roles,* 11, 61-78.

Fernandes, D. V., Canavarro, M. C., & Moreira, H. (2021). The role of mothers' self-compassion on mother- infant bonding during the COVID-19 pandemic: A longitudinal study exploring the mediating role of mindful parenting and parenting stress in the postpartum period. *Infant Mental Health Journal.* doi:10.1002/imhj.21942.

Fonseca, A., & Canavarro, M. C. (2017). Exploring the paths between dysfunctional attitudes towards motherhood and postpartum depressive symptoms: The moderating role of self-compassion. *Clinical Psychology & Psychotherapy,* 25(1), e96–e106. https://doi.org/10.1002/cpp.2145.

Foster, K., O'Brien, L., & Korhonen, T. (2011). Developing resilient children and families when parents have mental illness: A family-focused approach. *International Journal of Mental Health Nursing,* 21(1), 3–11. https://doi.org/10.1111/j.1447-0349.2011.00754.x.

Fuentes, M. J., Salas, M. D., Bernedo, I. M., & García-Martín, M. A. (2014). Impact of the parenting style of foster parents on the behaviour problems of foster children. *Child: Care, Health and Development,* 41(5), 704–711. doi:10.1111/cch.12215.

Garbacz, S. A., Herman, K. C., Thompson, A. M., & Reinke, W. M. (2017). Family engagement in education and intervention: Implementation and evaluation to maximize family, school, and student outcomes. *Journal of School Psychology,* 62, 1–10. https://doi.org/10.1016/j.jsp.2017.04.002.

Geurtzen, N., Scholte, R. H. J., Engels, R. C. M. E., Tak, Y. R., & van Zundert, R. M. P. (2014). Association between Mindful Parenting and Adolescents' Internalizing Problems: Non-judgmental Acceptance of Parenting as Core Element. *Journal of Child and Family Studies,* 24(4), 1117–1128. https://doi.org/10.1007/s10826-014-9920-9.

Gouveia, M. J., Carona, C., Canavarro, M. C., & Moreira, H. (2016). Self-Compassion and Dispositional Mindfulness Are Associated with Parenting Styles and Parenting Stress: the Mediating Role of Mindful Parenting. *Mindfulness,* 7(3), 700–712. doi:10.1007/s12671-016-0507-y.

Gulley, L. D., Oppenheimer, C. W., & Hankin, B. L. (2014). Associations among negative parenting, attention bias to anger, and social anxiety among youth. *Developmental Psychology,* 50(2), 577–585. https://doi.org/10.1037/a0033624.

Henderson, J. L., Brownlie, E. B., McMain, S., Chaim, G., Wolfe, D. A., Rush, B., Boritz, T., & Beitchman, J. H. (2017). Enhancing prevention and intervention for youth concurrent mental health and substance use disorders: The Research and Action for

Teens study. *Early Intervention in Psychiatry,* 13(1), 110– 119. https://doi.org/10.1111/eip.12458.

Hofmeyer, A., Taylor, R., & Kennedy, K. (2020). Knowledge for nurses to better care for themselves so they can better care for others during the Covid-19 pandemic and beyond. *Nurse Education Today,* 94, 104503.

Hollis-Walker, L., & Colosimo, K. (2011). Mindfulness, self-compassion, and happiness in non-meditators: A theoretical and empirical examination. *Personality and Individual differences*, *50*(2), 222-227.

Honey, A., Fraser, V., Llewellyn, G., Hazell, P., & Clarke, S. (2013). Parental influence on the mental health-related behaviour of young people with mental illness: Young people's perceptions. *Advances in Mental Health,* 12(1), 63–74. https://doi.org/10.5172/jamh.2013.12.1.63.

Jefferson, F. A., Shires, A., & McAloon, J. (2020). Parenting Self-compassion: a Systematic Review and Meta-analysis. *Mindfulness,* 11(9), 2067–2088. https://doi. org/10.1007/s12671-020-01401-x.

Johnson, E. A., & O'Brien, K. A. (2013). Self-Compassion Soothes the Savage EGO-Threat System: Effects on Negative Affect, Shame, Rumination, and Depressive Symptoms. *Journal of Social and Clinical Psychology,* 32(9), 939–963. https://doi.org/10.1521/jscp.2013.32.9.939.

Kabat-Zinn, J. (2003). Mindfulness-based interventions in context: Past, present, and future. *Clinical Psychology: Science and Practice,* 10(2), 144–156. https://doi.org/10.1093/clipsy.bpg016.

Kamis, C. (2020). The Long-Term Impact of Parental Mental Health on Children's Distress Trajectories in Adulthood. *Society and Mental Health,* 11(1), 54–68. https://doi.org/10.1177/2156869320912520.

Karney, B. R., & Bradbury, T. N. (2020). Research on marital satisfaction and stability in the 2010s: Challenging conventional wisdom. *Journal of Marriage and Family,* 82(1), 100–116.

Kessler, R. C., McLaughlin, K. A., Green, J. G., Gruber, M. J., Sampson, N. A., Zaslavsky, A. M., Aguilar- Gaxiola, S., Alhamzawi, A. O., Alonso, J., Angermeyer, M., Benjet, C., Bromet, E., Chatterji, S., de Girolamo, G., Demyttenaere, K., Fayyad, J., Florescu, S., Gal, G., Gureje, O., ... Williams, D. R. (2010). Childhood adversities and adult psychopathology in the WHO World Mental Health Surveys. *British Journal of Psychiatry,* 197(5), 378–385. https://doi.org/10.1192/bjp.bp.110.080499.

Khong, C., & Nhat, H. T. (2014). *Beginning anew: Four steps to restoring communication.* Parallax Press.

Kirby, J. N., & Baldwin, S. (2017). A Randomized Micro-trial of a Loving-Kindness Meditation to Help Parents Respond to Difficult Child Behavior Vignettes. *Journal of Child and Family Studies, 27*(5), 1614–1628. https://doi.org/10.1007/s10826-017-0989-9

Kohler, H.-P., J. R. Behrman and A. Skytthe. (2005). Partner + children = happiness? An assessment of the effect of fertility and partnerships on subjective well-being in Danish twins. *Population and Development Review* 31(3): 407-445.

Kwak, J. Y., Kim, J. Y., & Yoon, Y. W. (2018). Effect of parental neglect on smartphone addiction in adolescents in South Korea. *Child Abuse & Neglect,* 77, 75–84. doi:10.1016/j.chiabu.2017.12.0.

Kyriazos, T. and Stalikas, A. (2018) Positive Parenting or Positive Psychology Parenting? Towards a Conceptual Framework of Positive Psychology Parenting. *Psychology,* 9, 1761-1788. DOI:10.4236/psych.2018.97104.

Lara, L., & Saracostti, M. (2019). Effect of Parental Involvement on Children's Academic Achievement in Chile. *Frontiers in Psychology,* 10. https://doi.org/10.3389/fpsyg.2019.01464.

Lathren, C. R., Rao, S. S., Park, J., & Bluth, K. (2021). Self-Compassion and Current Close Interpersonal Relationships: A Scoping Literature Review. *Mindfulness,* 12(5), 1078–1093. doi:10.1007/s12671- 020-01566-5.

Lathren, C., Bluth, K., & Zvara, B. (2020). Parent Self-Compassion and Supportive Responses to Child Difficult Emotion: An Intergenerational Theoretical Model Rooted in Attachment. *Journal of family theory & review*, 12(3), 368–381. https://doi.org/10.1111/jftr.12388.

Le, N. H. G., Hsiao, C. T., & Heo, Y. (2020). Trans-cultural journeys of East-Asian educators: The impact of the three teachings. *International Journal for Cross-Disciplinary Subjects in Education, 11*(1), 4201- 4210.

Liss, M., & Erchull, M. J. (2015). Not hating what you see: Self-compassion may protect against negative mental health variables connected to self-objectification in college women. *Body Image,* 14, 5–12. https://doi.org/10.1016/j.bodyim.2015.02.006.

Maccoby, E. E. (2000). Parenting and its Effects on Children: On Reading and Misreading Behavior Genetics. *Annual Review of Psychology,* 51(1), 1–27. https://doi.org/10.1146/annurev.psych.51.1.1.

Manwell, L. A., Barbic, S. P., Roberts, K., Durisko, Z., Lee, C., Ware, E., & McKenzie, K. (2015). What is mental health? Evidence towards a new definition from a mixed-methods multidisciplinary international survey. *BMJ Open,* 5(6), e007079. https://doi.org/10.1136/bmjopen-2014-007079.

Maybery, D., Ling, L., Szakacs, E., & Reupert, A. (2005). Children of a parent with a mental illness: perspectives on need. *Australian E-Journal for the Advancement of Mental Health,* 4(2), 78–88. https://doi.org/10.5172/jamh.4.2.78.

Meadows, S. O., McLanahan, S. S., & Brooks-Gunn, J. (2007). Parental Depression and Anxiety and Early Childhood Behavior Problems Across Family Types. *Journal of Marriage and Family,* 69(5), 1162– 1177. https://doi.org/10.1111/j.1741-3737.2007.00439.x.

Mikolajczak M, Gross JJ, Roskam I. (2019). Parental Burnout: What Is It, and Why Does It Matter? *Clinical Psychological Science,* 7(6):1319-1329. doi:10.1177/2167702619858430.

Mikolajczak, M., & Roskam, I. (2018). A Theoretical and Clinical Framework for Parental Burnout: The Balance Between Risks and Resources (BR2). *Frontiers in Psychology,* 9. doi:10.3389/fpsyg.2018.00886.

Mikolajczak, M., Gross, J. J., & Roskam, I. (2019). Parental Burnout: What Is It, and Why Does It Matter? *Clinical Psychological Science*, 7(6), 1319–1329. https://doi.org/10.1177/2167702619858430.

Mikulincer, M., & Shaver, P. R. (2017). *Attachment in Adulthood, Second Edition: Structure, Dynamics, and Change* (Second edition). The Guilford Press.

Mitnick, D. M., Heyman, R. E., & Smith Slep, A. M. (2009). Changes in relationship satisfaction across the transition to parenthood: A meta-analysis. *Journal of Family Psychology,* 23(6), 848–852. https://doi.org/10.1037/a0017004.

Moreira, H., & Canavarro, M. C. (2018). The Association Between Self-Critical Rumination and Parenting Stress: The Mediating Role of Mindful Parenting. *Journal of Child and Family Studies, 27*(7), 2265– 2275. https://doi.org/10.1007/s10826-018-1072-x.

Moreira, H., Carona, C., Silva, N., Nunes, J., & Canavarro, M. C. (2015). Exploring the link between maternal attachment-related anxiety and avoidance and mindful parenting: The mediating role of self- compassion. *Psychology and Psychotherapy: Theory, Research, and Practice,* 89(4), 369–384.

Moreira, H., Gouveia, M. J., Carona, C., Silva, N., & Canavarro, M. C. (2014). Maternal Attachment and Children's Quality of Life: The Mediating Role of Self-compassion and Parenting Stress. *Journal of Child and Family Studies,* 24(8), 2332–2344. https://doi.org/10.1007/s10826-014-0036-z.

Murn, L. T., & Steele, M. R. (2019). What matters most? Age and gender differences in self-compassion and body attitudes among college students. *Counselling Psychology Quarterly,* 1–20. doi:10.1080/09515070.2019.1605.

NEFF, K. (2003b). Self-Compassion: An Alternative Conceptualization of a Healthy Attitude Toward Oneself. *Self and Identity,* 2(2), 85–101. https://doi.org/10.1080/15298860309032.

Neff, K. D. (2003a). The development and validation of a scale to measure self-compassion. *Self and identity*, *2*(3), 223-250.

Neff, K. D. (2011). Self-compassion, self-esteem, and well-being. *Social and personality psychology compass*, *5*(1), 1-12.

Neff, K. D., & Germer, C. K. (2012). A Pilot Study and Randomized Controlled Trial of the Mindful Self- Compassion Program. *Journal of Clinical Psychology,* 69(1), 28–44. https://doi.org/10.1002/jclp.21923.

Neff, K. D., Long, P., Knox, M. C., Davidson, O., Kuchar, A., Costigan, A., Williamson, Z., Rohleder, N., Tóth-Király, I., & Breines, J. G. (2018). The forest and the trees: Examining the association of self- compassion and its positive and negative components with psychological functioning. *Self and Identity,* 17(6), 627–645. https://doi.org/10.1080/15298868.2018.1436587.

Nelson, S. K., Kushlev, K., English, T., Dunn, E. W., & Lyubomirsky, S. (2013). In defense of parenthood: Children are associated with more joy than misery. *Psychological Science,* 24, 3-10.

Nguyen, T. M., & Le, G. N. H. (2021). The influence of COVID-19 stress on psychological well-being among Vietnamese adults: The role of self-compassion and gratitude. *Traumatology, 27*(1), 86-97.

Nguyen, T. M., Bui, T. T. H., Xiao, X., & Le, V. H. (2020). The Influence of Self-Compassion on Mindful Parenting: A Mediation Model of Gratitude. *The Family Journal,* 28(4), 455–462. doi:10.1177/1066480720950421.

Nguyen, T. M., Xiao, X., Xiong, S., Guo, C., & Cheng, G. (2020). Effects of parental educational involvement on classroom peer status among Chinese primary school students: A moderated mediation model of psychological Suzhi and family socioeconomic status. *Children and Youth Services Review,* 111, 104881. doi:10.1016/j.childyouth.2020.

Nhat, H. T. (2018, December 31). Beginning anew. *Lion's Roar: Buddhist Wisdom for our Time*. https://www.lionsroar.com/beginning-anew/

Park, S., & Holloway, S. D. (2016). The effects of school-based parental involvement on academic achievement at the child and elementary school level: A longitudinal study. *The Journal of Educational Research,* 110(1), 1–16. https://doi.org/10.1080/00220671.2015.1016600.

Pepping, C. A., Davis, P. J., O'Donovan, A., & Pal, J. (2014). Individual Differences in Self-Compassion: The Role of Attachment and Experiences of Parenting in Childhood. *Self and Identity,* 14(1), 104– 117. doi:10.1080/15298868.2014.9550.

Psychogiou, L., Legge, K., Parry, E., Mann, J., Nath, S., Ford, T., & Kuyken, W. (2016). Self-compassion and parenting in mothers and fathers with depression. *Mindfulness,* 7, 896–908. https://doi.org/10.1007/s12671-016-0528-6.

Rangganadhan, A. R., & Todorov, N. (2010). Personality and Self-Forgiveness: The Roles of Shame, Guilt, Empathy and Conciliatory Behavior. *Journal of Social and Clinical Psychology,* 29(1), 1–22. https://doi.org/10.1521/jscp.2010.29.1.1.

relationship satisfaction across the transition to parenthood: A meta-analysis. *Journal of Family Psychology,* 23(6), 848–852. DOI:10.1037/a0017004.

Reupert, A. E., J Maybery, D., & Kowalenko, N. M. (2013). Children whose parents have a mental illness: prevalence, need and treatment. *Medical Journal of Australia,* 199(S3). https://doi.org/10.5694/mja11.11200.

Roskam, I., Brianda, M. E., & Mikolajczak, M. (2018). A Step Forward in the Conceptualization and Measurement of Parental Burnout: The Parental Burnout Assessment (PBA). *Frontiers in Psychology,* 9. https://doi.org/10.3389/fpsyg.2018.00758.

Ross, T. R. (2016). The differential effects of parental involvement on high school completion and postsecondary attendance. *Education Policy Analysis Archives,* 24, 30. https://doi.org/10.14507/epaa.24.2030.

Roy F. Baumeister, Kathleen D. Vohs, Jennifer L. Aaker & Emily N. Garbinsky. (2013). Some key differences between a happy life and a meaningful life, *The Journal of Positive Psychology,* 8:6, 505-516, DOI: 10.1080/17439760.2013.830764.

Ruud, T., Maybery, D., Reupert, A., Weimand, B., Foster, K., Grant, A., Skogøy, B. E., & Ose, S. O. (2019). Adult Mental Health Outpatients Who Have Minor Children: Prevalence of Parents, Referrals of Their Children, and Patient Characteristics. *Frontiers in Psychiatry,* 10. https://doi.org/10.3389/fpsyt.2019.00163

Schepman, K., Collishaw, S., Gardner, F., Maughan, B., Scott, J., & Pickles, A. (2011). Do changes in parent mental health explain trends in youth emotional problems? *Social*

Science & Medicine, 73(2), 293– 300. https://doi.org/10.1016/j.socscimed.2011.05.015.

Shewark, E. A., Ramos, A. M., Liu, C., Ganiban, J. M., Fosco, G., Shaw, D. S., Reiss, D., Natsuaki, M. N., Leve, L. D., & Neiderhiser, J. M. (2021). The role of child negative emotionality in parenting and child adjustment: Gene-environment interplay. *Journal of Child Psychology and Psychiatry,* 62(12), 1453– 1461. https://doi.org/10.1111/jcpp.13420.

Sirois, F. M., Bögels, S., & Emerson, L. M. (2018). Self-compassion Improves Parental Well-being in Response to Challenging Parenting Events. *The Journal of Psychology,* 153(3), 327–341. https://doi.org/10.1080/00223980.2018.1523123.

Smallen, D., Eller, J., Rholes, W. S., & Simpson, J. A. (2021, August 9). Perceptions of Partner Responsiveness Across the Transition to Parenthood. *Journal of Family Psychology*. Advance online publication. http://dx.doi.org/10.1037/fam0000907.

Sorkkila, M., & Aunola, K. (2019). Risk Factors for Parental Burnout among Finnish Parents: The Role of Socially Prescribed Perfectionism. *Journal of Child and Family Studies,* 29(3), 648–659. https://doi.org/10.1007/s10826-019-01607-1.

Tangney, J. P., & Tracy, J. L. (2012). Self-conscious emotions. In *Handbook of self and identity* (pp. 446– 478). NY: Guilford Press.

Tárraga García, V., García Fernández, B., & Ruiz-Gallardo, J. R. (2017). Home-based family involvement and academic achievement: a case study in primary education. *Educational Studies,* 44(3), 361–375. https://doi.org/10.1080/03055698.2017.1373636.

Van Dam, N. T., Sheppard, S. C., Forsyth, J. P., & Earleywine, M. (2011). Self-compassion is a better predictor than mindfulness of symptom severity and quality of life in mixed anxiety and depression. *Journal of Anxiety Disorders,* 25(1), 123–130. https://doi.org/10.1016/j.janxdis.2010.08.011.

Voci, A., Veneziani, C. A., & Fuochi, G. (2019). Relating mindfulness, heartfulness, and psychological well- being: the role of self-compassion and gratitude. *Mindfulness,* 10(2), 339-351.

West, K. K., Mathews, B. L., & Kerns, K. A. (2013). Mother-child attachment and cognitive performance in middle childhood: An examination of mediating mechanisms. *Early Childhood Research Quarterly*, 28(2), 259–270. https://doi.org/10.1016/j.ecresq.2012.07.005.

Wilson, S., & Durbin, C. E. (2010). Effects of paternal depression on fathers' parenting behaviors: A meta- analytic review. *Clinical Psychology Review*, *30*(2), 167–180. https://doi.org/10.1016/j.cpr.2009.10.007.

Wolicki, S. B., Bitsko, R. H., Cree, R. A., Danielson, M. L., Ko, J. Y., Warner, L., & Robinson, L. R. (2021). Mental Health of Parents and Primary Caregivers by Sex and Associated Child Health Indicators. *Adversity and Resilience Science,* 2(2), 125–139. https://doi.org/10.1007/s42844-021-00037-7.

Wood, A. M., Joseph, S., & Maltby, J. (2009). Gratitude predicts psychological well-being above the Big Five facets. *Personality and Individual differences,* 46(4), 443-447.

World Health Organization. (2003). *Investing in Mental health.* https://www.who.int/mental_health/media/investing_mnh.pdf.

World Health Organization. (2014). *Mental health: a state of well-being*. World Health Organization. http://www.who.int/features/factfiles/mental_health/en/

Yarnell, L. M., Stafford, R. E., Neff, K. D., Reilly, E. D., Knox, M. C., & Mullarkey, M. (2015). Meta- Analysis of Gender Differences in Self-Compassion. *Self and Identity*, 14(5), 499–520. doi:10.1080/15298868.2015.1029966.

Chapter 5

A State-Trait Approach to Self-Compassion: Is It a Schema or a State of Mind?

Bruno Faustino
Lusófona University, Hei-Lab, Lisbon/Portugal
Faculty of Psychology of the University of Lisbon, Lisbon/Portugal

Abstract

Self-compassion has been described as an adaptive psychological domain that allows individuals to be kind to themselves and to others when confronted with personal flaws and inadequacies. In the face of a situation of suffering caused by oneself or/and others, self-compassion facilitates feelings of warmth, caring and affection, which signal an emotional need to overcome emotional distress. Previous research has associated self-compassion with psychological well-being, life satisfaction and psychological flexibility, and the regulation of psychological needs, suggesting that self-compassion can be seen as an adaptive self-domain. In addition, self-compassion measured as a psychological trait was associated with mindfulness and self-acceptance traits, and measured as a state of mind, was associated with early maladaptive schemas. In this sense, self-compassion can function as both: a psychological trait and a state. However, this distinction does not seem clear. Therefore, this chapter aims to contribute to that clarification by reviewing recent findings from a trait/state perspective based on a development schema theory combined with a state of mind approach. Suggestions for future research are also outlined to clarify whether self-compassion might be better conceptualized as a trait and/or as psychological state.

Keywords: self-compassion; psychological schemas; states of mind

In: The Importance of Self-Efficacy and Self-Compassion
Editor: James J. Carmona
ISBN: 978-1-68507-763-1

1. Introduction

Interest in self-compassion has grown exponentially over the past ten years, giving rise to a large number of scientific publications. These publications supported several meta-analytic studies that explore the relationships between self-compassion and coping (Ewert et al., 2021), self-compassion and self-efficacy (Liao et al., 2021), self-compassion and psychopathology (MacBeth & Gumley, 2012) and the effectiveness of self-compassion and related third-generation cognitive-behavioral therapies (Wilson et al., 2019), just to name a few. However, the notion of self-compassion (and mindfulness) has been around for over 2500 years and is rooted in the traditional Buddhist philosophy (Neff & Germer, 2012). In the Buddhist tradition compassion can be described as the "heartfelt wish that sentient beings be free from suffering and the causes of suffering (Hopkins, 2001)". This "heartfelt wish" along with loving-kindness, sympathetic joy and equanimity constituted the brahma-viharas, which are regarded as four sublime mental states that can be pursued through personal growth and development (Hofmann et al., 2011).

The notion that self-compassion can be achieved through personal development and/or self-compassion training (Gilbert, 2009), may support the notion that self-compassion can be a state of mind that individuals can achieve through experience. Thus, the compassionate mind training from the Compassion Focused-Therapy (CFT, Gilbert, 2005; 2014) is based on this premise. However, several studies suggest that compassion for others is a psychological trait distinct from compassion because they have roots in different evolutionary systems of emotion (Goetz et al., 2010). According to Gilbert (2014), compassion emerged as a social mentality based on three evolutionary systems (e.g., caring and nurturing), where individuals can feel compassion towards others, from others to themselves and towards themselves (self-compassion). In this sense, compassion can be seen as the central trait/domain, while compassion for others can be seen as a second-order trait. Furthermore, if self-compassion is an emergent property of several evolutionary emotional systems, it is more likely to be defined as a psychological trait.

A psychological trait describes a set of dispositional tendencies (e.g., cognition, emotion, behavior, needs) that are stable individual characteristics, while psychological states are context-dependent internal volatile mental characteristics (Geiser et al., 2017). The interest in the conceptualization of psychological variables as states and/or traits can be objectively measured in scientific databases. The term "state-trait" in the international database PsychINF returned 9,044 hits between 2010 and 2016 (Geiser et al., 2017). According to Deinzer and colleagues (1995), many psychological variables may contain both dimensions of state-trait features based on several degrees. For instance, on extreme measurements of hormone levels and mood individuals may show higher features of state-like psychological domains, while in the measure of intelligence or ability skills individuals may show higher features of trait-like psychological domains (Geiser et al., 2017). Probably, most psychological variables may have state components and trait-like characteristics that make clear differentiation difficult, especially when it comes to self-compassion.

Typically, clinicians use therapeutic strategies and tasks according to the specificity of the psychological construct that is being "worked on." The importance of differentiating trait from state when it comes to self-compassion can be emphasized by the need to choose the more adequate clinical strategy. Clinicians can choose to use stage-process approach to work with trait-like features and/or a moment-to-moment approach to work with state-like features of compassion. This will be explained further. Also, the present theoretical exploration of this dichotomy will be based on the Dialectical Core Schema Theory (or, in short, Dialectical Schema Theory, DST, Faustino, 2022, in press) and on a state of mind approach (Horowitz, 1987). But first, I will briefly review the definitions and the most influential authors devoted to the study of self-compassion.

2. The Basics of Self-Compassion

According to Neff (2003), self-compassion is an attitude relevant for every self-experience of suffering that encompasses six main elements articulated dialectally: Self-kindness vs. Self-judgment, Common humanity vs. Isolation and Mindfulness vs. Over-identification. Self-kindness means treating the self with warmness, tenderness and understanding when confronting emotional suffering instead of being harsh and judgmental towards the self. A sense of common humanity implies a shared view where one's failures and painful experiences belong to the nature of what means to be human, instead of feeling isolated and alienated from others (humanity). Mindfulness implies the maintenance of a balanced awareness of difficult/painful experiences rather an over-identifying with painful thoughts and emotions (Neff, 2003). This definition may blend different mental elements, where Self-kindness vs. Self-judgment may be regarded as attitudes towards the self; Common humanity vs. Isolation may be more related to core beliefs about the world, and Mindfulness vs. Over-identification may be regarded as cognitive abilities. In this sense, Neff's conceptualization of self-compassion encompasses several mental elements defining it as a complex construct. Can these mental elements be viewed as psychological traits? Nevertheless, this conceptualization of self-compassion is one of the most investigated due to the development of the self-compassion scale (SCS, 2003) which is translated into more than 18 languages, disseminating widely this instrument.

As stated before, there is a slightly different approach to self-compassion. In CFT, self-compassion is viewed from an evolutionary psychological perspective, and it is understood in terms of specific skills and attributes. According to Gilbert (2014), CFT evolved from the recognition that: (1) the human brain is a product of evolution, (2) the human brain is shaped for processing social interaction (3) self-self-relationships (e.g., self-shame), may impair mental health, (4) recent cognitive abilities may influence and be influenced by social motives developed in an early stage and (5) compassion training may have several psychological and physiological benefits. Also, Gilbert (2014) stated that psychopathological domains may be associated with basic motivational systems (sex, status, attachment), which organize mind elements and guide behavior to avoid threats and seek specific rewards. These are the fundamentals of social mentalities.

Social mentalities are the evolved mindsets that stem from the motivational systems for interpersonal relating and are typically described as competing and social rank, cooperating/sharing, caring and nurturing and seeking and responding to care (Gilbert, 2014). Aligned with this, humans have three types of affect regulation systems (threat-protection system, seeking positive emotions and affiliative focuses soothing) that form basic motives that humans engage towards the self and others (Gilbert, 2014). In this sense, humans tend to be driven by these systems that motivate different mindsets and behaviors which are related to avoiding threats, searching for pleasure activities, seeking social support/soothing and engaging in prosocial behaviors (Gilbert, 2010). Self-compassion emerges from the interaction of these emotional systems rooted in evolutionary motives. The multimodal compassionate mind training determines that individuals may develop specific attributes (e.g., sensitivity, empathy, distress tolerance) and skills (e.g., attention, imagery, and reasoning) to cultivate an internal compassionate relationship with themselves which may replace self-criticism, self-blame and condemning (see Gilbert, 2010 for details). To be compassionate towards oneself requires developing a set of features that stem out of major developmental emotion regulation systems, which help individuals to be less self-critical, self-punitive and self-loathing.

Furthermore, research seems to support these theoretical claims. Self-compassion measured by the SCS, on one hand, seems to be positively associated with social connectivity, happiness, personal initiative, extroversion, optimism, exploration and conscientiousness (Neff et al., 2005), psychological well-being (Lopez et al., 2018; Zessin et al., 2015) and with self-acceptance, mindfulness and with the regulation of psychological needs (Faustino et al., 2020). On the other hand, self-compassion seems to be negatively associated with generic symptomatology, anxiety, self-criticism and depressive symptoms (Faustino et al., 2020; Costa & Pinto-Gouveia, 2011; Raes, 2011; Gilbert, et al., 2011; Neff et al., 2005).

3. A Developmental and Dialectical Core Schema Theory of Self-Compassion

Schema theorists rely on the information processing paradigm of human cognition to explain and conceptualize how information is perceived, stored and recalled in the mind. A schema may be described as an abstract mental structure that encompasses several elements of the experience (e.g., cognition, emotion, physical sensations) that tend to guide human motivation and behavior (Beck et al., 1979, Young et al., 2003). Schemas are viewed as experience-based abstractions that encompass emotional meaning that is learned due to relational interactions. According to Young and colleagues (2003), humans tend to develop early maladaptive schemas (EMS) in childhood and adolescence due to the frustration of core emotional needs, which are secure attachment, adequate autonomy and performance, adequate internal and external limits, assertiveness and spontaneity/adequate expression (Young et al., 2003). EMSs are seen as trait-like structures that emerge from the dysfunctional meaning associated with emotional pain from experiences of emotional trauma and deprivation, neglect, submission and punishment. Schemas are responsible for the way in which individuals see themselves, others, the world and the future (Beck et al., 1979, Young et al., 2003), which means that relational experiences with significant others may play a role in how individuals develop stable worldviews. Recent research showed systematic relationships between early maladaptive schemas with difficulties in the regulation of psychological needs (Faustino & Vasco, 2020a,b,c).

Recently, Faustino (2022, in press), purposed the Dialectical Core Schema Theory (or, in short, Dialectical Schema Theory, DST), which states that individuals not only develop dysfunctional cognitions about the self and others (e.g., maladaptive schemas) but also develop adaptive schemas based on adaptive emotional and relational experiences through life cycles and stages. Even though this notion is not innovative (see Beck et al, 1979), a coherent theoretical and empirical articulation between maladaptive and adaptive schemas has not been made.

Briefly, DST (Faustino, 2022, in press) states that individuals tend to develop not only maladaptive schemas based on relational toxic experiences throughout the entire life cycle (e.g., developmental stages from early childhood to adulthood) but also tend to develop adaptive schemas based on the adaptive experiences. In this sense, if individuals develop a maladaptive core schema, the opposite schema tends also to be developed (Faustino, 2022). Therefore, schemas may be conceptualized in dialectical poles. Also, dialectical schemas may be developed not only due to emotional relational experiences but also through cognitive processing (e.g., thinking about a situation and developing a core belief), social messages (e.g., media exposure), selective internalization of traits (e.g., adopting the attitudes of a role model) and through emotional learnings towards the self and others (e.g., through reward and punishments).

In this sense, "*Contradictory adaptive and maladaptive core schemas may be present in the information processing cascade when they are evoked and/or activated through internal and/or external stimuli. Contradictory core schemas may both be activated at the same time, leading to internal conflicts causing difficulties in the decision-making process*" (pp. 9, Faustino, in press). For instance, if an individual has both self-representations of "I only see defects in myself" (maladaptive core schema) and "I can see virtues and flaws in myself "(adaptive core schema), and both representations are equally activated due to an experience of abandonment/rejection, individuals may feel conflicted, confused, numb and/or ambivalent to process the emotional experience. It is the activation of both maladaptive and adaptive core schemas that lie at the core of the internal conflict. In this sense, "*This perspective emphasizes the conflictual and dimensional nature of the human mind where individuals tend to swing back and forth on a psychological continuum between adaptive and maladaptive core schemas, which are articulated dialectically. Therefore, individuals hold contradictory information about themselves and others which is embedded in core schemas*" (pp. 9, Faustino, in press).

Based on the DST perspective if individuals hold adaptive and maladaptive cognitions about the self and others, it is important to explore how this relates to self-compassion. Within an integrative perspective, self-compassion encompasses several elements that may be conceptualized as attitudes (e.g., self-kindness vs. self-judgment), attributes (e.g., sensitivity, empathy, distress tolerance), and skills (e.g., attention, imagery, and reasoning), which resembles an extremely complex domain or a social mentality – see the Theoretical Integration section further). However, based on Neff's perspective, self-compassion seems to be composed of three attitudinal dialectical domains. Schemas are the structures that hold core beliefs, assumptions, attributes, and expectations that influence attitudinal dispositions about the self and others. This means that a dispositional attitude and the experience of self-compassion may be dependent on the underlying core schemas that are activated. In fact, some research suggests this effect.

Self-compassion measured by the SCS showed negative associations with EMS and mediated the associations between EMSs and psychological distress (Thimm, 2017). In another study, self-compassion was negatively correlated with emotional schemas (i.e., maladaptive views of emotional experience) and mediated both models of the relationships between emotional schemas and symptomatology and between emotional schemas and the regulation of psychological needs (Faustino et al., 2020). Thus, emotional schemas seems to play a mediational role in emotion regulation (Faustino & Vasco, 2021). Despite being few, taken together these results suggest that self-compassion is closely related to schematic functioning. Nevertheless, one research paper seems to shed some light on this issue. An experimental study divided into 4 experiments where individuals were engaged in several tasks related to the activation of *support-giving schemas*, found that giving support and thinking about giving support increased the state of self-compassion (Breines & Chen, 2013. Authors point out that contextual schemas … "*for receiving support and acceptance influence self-treatment, schemas related to giving support to others appear to influence self-compassion, an adaptive form of self-treatment*" (pp.5, Breines & Chen, 2013). One issue that can be studied is the differentiation related to the typology of schemas. This study is currently ongoing. However, it is important to explore how self-compassion relates to the concept of *states of mind* that are more related to context-dependent shifting constructs.

4. States of Mind Approach to Self-Compassion

States of Mind are forms of subjective experience that cluster activated mental elements such as cognitions, feelings, needs, and/or somatic sensations that tend to guide motivated action tendencies and behavior (Faustino et al., 2021; Horowitz, 1987). States of mind may also be regarded as transient mental modules that encompass several forms of experience. These states may be laden with adaptive or with maladaptive emotions associated with emotional suffering. Adaptive and maladaptive schemas are regarded as psychological *traits*, which means that they tend to have a dispositional activation, while states of mind are context-dependent states. One major aspect of the notion of the concept of states of mind is the activation of the *underlying themes* which characterize these transient states (Dimaggio et al., 2015; Faustino et al., 2021). For instance, a maladaptive schema typically only encompass one dysfunctional psychological theme (e.g., abandonment or emotional deprivation), while a state of mind, typically involves the concomitant activation of several schemas with a *trait-like* disposition sharing similar dysfunctional themes (e.g., activation at the same time of schemas such as defectiveness, unworthy and subjugation). In this sense, a fragile, weak, or vulnerable state of mind emerges in the flow of consciousness, guiding individuals' emotions and behavior. States of mind are a construct similar to schema modes (Young et al., 2003). However, a theoretical differentiation can be made. Based on both definitions, where states of mind are seen as forms of subjective experience and schema modes are the association of EMS and coping responses, it appears that schema modes are more related to operant and external behavior, while states of mind seem to be more related to inner private experience (Faustino et al., 2021). However, this distinction remains theoretical.

In the development of the States of Mind Questionnaire (SMQ, Faustino, et al., 2021), several states of mind were conceptualized in four major domains: fragile states, coping states, egosintonic states and self-care states. In this chapter, I will only focus on the domain of the self-care states. In this domain, four states of mind were conceptualized. A state of *attachment and belonging/interpersonal safeness* representing a state of connectivity and feeling of belonging with others; a state of *self-trust and integrity/assertiveness*, representing a sense of cohesion, self-reliance, and integrity; a state of *acceptance and forgiveness/mindfulness*, representing a state of self-acceptance and mindfulness; and a state of *self-worth and compassion/emotional fulfillment*, representing a state of self-compassion and emotional fulfillment. This last state of mind tried to capture the notion of self-worth which is intrinsically related to the ability to be compassionate towards the self and the concomitant emotional fulfillment that may be associated.

Research with the SMQ showed that the state of *self-worth and compassion/emotional fulfillment* was negatively correlated with all EMS and associated schema domains and was negatively correlated with all symptomatic domains of the Brief Symptomatic Inventory (BSI, Canavarro, 1999). The state of *self-worth and compassion/emotional fulfillment* showed the strongest negative correlations with EMS from the disconnection and rejection domain (e.g., mistrust/abuse), impaired autonomy domain (e.g., failure) and with overprotection and inhibition domain (e.g., pessimism). Also, the self-care states domain was the best predictor of the overall symptomatology and the state of *self-worth and compassion/emotional fulfillment* was the best predictor of the overall symptomatology when compared with the other adaptive states of mind (Faustino et al., 2021). Taken together this evidence seems to suggest that self-compassion as measured by the SMQ, operates in an opposite direction of the maladaptive schematic functioning and it is possible to measure what is contained in a complex state of mind.

5. Theoretical Integration

Based on this literature review, can we define self-compassion as a psychological trait or a state? It is now clear that there are no definitive conclusions, but several open hypotheses. From an evolutionary perspective, humans developed several social mentalities based on several interpersonal motivational systems (e.g., caring and nurturing) that predispose individuals to develop several social roles (Gilbert, 2014). Different social mentalities organize and predispose an individual´s mind to process congruent information. For example, seeing somebody crying can be pleasurable if I am motivated to hurt (e.g., competing interpersonal system), but it can be distressing if I am motivated to care (caring and nurturing system). Thus, according to Gilbert (2014), self-compassion emerges as a social mentality linked to motives, emotions, and abilities to be supportive, caring, kind and understanding towards the self (and others). Despite some differences, this notion is not opposed to the notion of core emotional needs (Young et al., 2003).

From a schematic perspective, individuals develop personal worldviews based on the developed core cognitions about the self and others that stem from the interaction between experience and genetics (Almeida, 2021; Beck et al., 1979). Adaptive and maladaptive core schemas tend to be developed during the life cycle through several mechanisms (e.g., emotional experience, cognitive processing) becoming enduring traits that are articulated dialectically (Faustino, 2022). Research suggests that early toxic experiences tend to lead to stronger development of early maladaptive schemas (Young et al., 2003), which means that early infant-adult interactions play a role in adults' worldview. These toxic experiences are related to the frustration of core emotional needs (Young et al., 2003). However, it is likely to assume that individuals also tend to have early adaptive experiences fostering the development of early adaptive schemas (Lockwood and Young, 2012).

In this sense, during childhood or adolescence if individuals interact with caregivers and peers who are compassionate, caring and accepting it is likely that individuals will develop adaptive core schemas, "I am a lovable person", or "I accept myself as I am" that may foster compassion towards the self. Thus, if these healthy experiences are systematically repeated, individuals may develop a stable sense of self that is worthy of affection, care, attention, love and is socially desired. In this sense, early experiences related to emotional needs (e.g., secure attachment) driven by the interpersonal motivational systems (e.g., caring and nurturing) may lead to the development of adaptive core schemas that may contribute to the mentality of compassion, probably with trait-like features.

Although dispositional self-compassion seems to make sense based on the previous theorizing, research suggests that self-compassion can also be thought of as a state (Breines & Chen, 2013; Faustino et al., 2021). If self-compassion can also be studied as a psychological state, based on the concept of states of mind described above, self-compassion may be dependent on the concomitant activation of its underlying mental elements, which were defined in the SMQ as self-worth and compassion/emotional fulfillment. These mental elements represent adaptive views of the self and the felt sense of emotional fulfillment that invades the somatic domain of the human body when this state is triggered. States of mind are moment-to-moment complex constructs that are activated based on contextual demands. This means that the state of self-worth and compassion/emotional fulfillment tend to be contextually dependent and are rooted in situations. The complex nature of states of mind is similar to Neff's′ notion of self-compassion because it also describes a cluster of different mental elements gathered thematically. Thus, this notion is not so far away from the notion of Gilbert's social mentality because it also articulates interpersonal motives, attributes and skills of compassion.

These theoretical claims may contribute to clinical decision-making process, which can be based on a stage-process approach to work with trait-like features and/or a moment-to-moment approach to work with state-like features of the absence of compassion. Core schemas are the structural templates to "read the world" and if an individual has a harsh, punitive, pessimistic and destructive view of the self and others, which is the opposite of a compassionate worldview, a stage-process approach can be a suitable choice. On one hand, stage-process approaches tend to help individuals to follow specific therapeutic tasks based on stage aims (e.g., exploring childhood patterns - conscious awareness, (stage one), understanding cause-effects impacts - cognitive reattribution (stage 2)), leading to schema restructuring (see Young et al., 2003 and Beck et al., 1979, for details). On the other hand, a moment-to-moment approach tends to be focused on distressing volatile emotional states associated with difficult feelings, emotions and needs. If an individual manifests feelings of self-depreciation and vulnerability at a given moment, a moment-to-moment self-affirmation task can be promoted by the therapist with the aim of facilitating emotional relief and compassion (see Greenberg and Goldman, 2017 for details). In this sense, both strategies can be used based on the specific manifestations of the lack of self-compassion.

Finally, and completing the above integration attempt, early experiences associated with emotional needs (e.g., secure attachment) and driven by interpersonal motivational systems (e.g., caring and nurturing) can lead to the development of adaptive core schemas that can contribute to the compassion mindset, which may exhibit trait-like or state-like characteristics framed contextually.

6. Future Research

Future experimental research may focus attention on differentiating between various mental elements that are embedded in conceptualizations of compassion and how they can be optimized. For example, it would be interesting to explore how individuals respond to self-assessment compassion questionnaires after being primed with various emotionally-charged scenarios. Clinical research may be focused on the enhancement of therapeutic strategies regarding the stimulation of trait and state-like construct of self-compassion. Finally, psychometric studies of the existing instruments and the development of new ones may also be of value to continue to measure and explore self-compassion.

Conclusion

Self-compassion is a complex psychological construct that surpasses the dichotomy of trait and state. From Buddhist traditions to evolutionary psychology, self-compassion emerges as one of the most studied psychological domains in the past years, which reveals interest by researchers and clinicians. Self-compassion can be associated with adaptive core schemas as they shape how individuals see themselves and the world in an adaptive manner. From a states of mind perspective, self-compassion may encompass several recurring mental elements which are adaptive signaling feelings of warmth, caring, affection, which may soothe emotional distress. Self-compassion may assume different manifestations depending on individual's specificities, exhibiting trait-like or state-like features. In this sense, clinical decision-making should be based on specific individual's manifestations of compassion, which means having a stage-process approach to work with trait-like features and/or a moment-to-moment approach to work with state-like features of compassion.

References

Almeida, V. B. F. (2021). *Evidence-Based Clinical Decision-Making: Conceptual and Empirical Foundations for an Integrative Psychological and Neurobiological*

Transtheoretical Metamodel. Doctoral Theisis in Clinical Psychology. University of Lisbon.

Beck, A. T., Rush, A. J., Shaw, B., & Emery, G. (1979). *Cognitive therapy of depression.* New York: Guilford Press.

Breines, J. G., & Chen, S. (2013). Activating the inner caregiver: The role of support-giving schemas in increasing state self-compassion. *Journal of Experimental Social Psychology, 49*(1), 58–64. https://doi.org/10.1016/j.jesp.2012.07.015

Canavarro, M. C. (1999). Inventário de sintomas psicopatológicos – BSI. In M. R. Simões, M. Gonçalves, L. S. Almeida (Eds.), *Testes e Provas Psicológicas em Portugal* (Vol. II, pp.95-109). [*Inventory of psychopathological symptoms*]. Braga: APPORT/SHO.

Costa, J., & Pinto-Gouveia, J. (2011). Acceptance of pain. Self-compassion and psychopathology: Using the Chronic Pain Acceptance Questionnaire to identify patients' subgroups. *Clinical Psychology and Psychotherapy, 18,* 292–302. doi:10.1002/cpp.718.

Deinzer, R., Steyer, R., Eid, M., Notz, P., Schwenkmezger, P., Ostendorf, F., & Neubauer, A. (1995). Situational effects in trait assessment: The FPI, NEOFFI and EPI questionnaires. *European Journal of Personality, 9,* 1–23.

Dimaggio, G., Montano, A., Popolo, R., & Salvatore G. (2015). *Metacognitive Interpersonal Therapy for personality disorders.* London: Taylor & Francis.

Ewert, C., Vater, A.M., & Schröder–Abé, M. (2021). Self-Compassion and Coping: a Meta-Analysis. *Mindfulness, 12*, 1063-1077. https://doi.org/10. 1007/s12671-020-01563-8.

Faustino, B. & Vasco, A. B. (2020a). Relationships between emotional processing difficulties and early maladaptive schemas on the regulation of psychological needs. *Clinical Psychology and Psychotherapy, 27*(6), 804-813. https://doi.org/10. 1002/cpp.2464

Faustino, B. & Vasco, A. B. (2020b). Schematic functioning, interpersonal dysfunctional cycles, and cognitive fusion in the complementary paradigmatic perspective: Analysis of a clinical sample. *Journal of Contemporary Psychotherapy, 1*(50), 47–55. https://doi.org/10.1007/s10879-019-09422-x

Faustino, B. & Vasco, A. B. (2020b). Early maladaptive schemas and cognitive fusion on the regulation of psychological needs. *Journal of Contemporary Psychotherapy, 1*(50), 105–112. https://doi.org/10.1007/s10879-019-09446-3

Faustino, B., Vasco, A. B., Silva, A. N., & Marques, T. (2020). Relationships between emotional schemas, mindfulness, self-compassion and unconditional self-acceptance on the regulation of psychological needs. *Research in Psychotherapy: Psychopathology, Process and Outcome, 23*(2), 145-156. doi:10.4081/ripppo.2020. 442.

Faustino, B., & Vasco, A. B. (2021). Emotional schemas mediate the relationship between emotion regulation and symptomatology. *Current Psychology: A Journal for Diverse Perspectives on Diverse Psychological Issues.* Advance online publication. https://doi.org/10.1007/s12144-021-01560-7

Faustino, B., Vasco, A. B., Dimaggio, G., da Silva, A. N., & Seromenho, S. (2021). Self-assessment of patterns of subjective experience: development and psychometric study of the States of Mind Questionnaire. *Research in Psychotherapy: Psychopathology, Process and Outcome*, *23*(3), 320-340. doi: 10.4081/ripppo.2020.465.

Faustino, B. (2022). Maladaptive and Adaptive Cognitions about the Self and Others: Confirmatory Factor Analysis of the Brief Core Schemas Scales. *Psychological Reports*. https://doi.org/10.1177/00332941211063602.

Faustino, B. (in press). Introducing Dialectical Core Schemas Theory through Mediation Models. *International peer review journal.*

Geiser, C., Götz, T., Preckel, F., & Freund, P. A. (2017). States and traits: Theories, models, and assessment. *European Journal of Psychological Assessment, 33*(4), 219–223. https://doi.org/10.1027/1015-5759/a000413.

Gilbert, P. (2010). *Compassion focused therapy: distinctive features. The CBT distinctive features series*. London; New York: Routledge. ISBN 9780415448079. OCLC 463971957.

Gilbert, P. (2014). The origins and nature of compassion focused therapy. *British Journal of Clinical Psychology*, *53*(1), 6-41. https://doi.org/10.1111/ bjc.12043.

Gilbert, P. (Ed.). (2005). *Compassion: Conceptualizations, research and use in psychotherapy*. New York, NY, US: Routledge.

Gilbert, P., McEwan, K., Matos, M., & Rivis, A. (2011). Fears of compassion: Development of three self-report measures. *Psychology & Psychotherapy: Theory, Research and Practice*, 84(3), 239-255. doi:10.1348/147 608310X526511.

Goetz, J. L., Keltner, D., & Simon-Thomas, E. (2010). Compassion: an evolutionary analysis and empirical review. *Psychological bulletin*, *136*(3), 351–374. https://doi.org/10.1037/a0018807.

Greenberg, L. S., & Goldman, R. N. (2019). Theory of practice of emotion-focused therapy. In L. S. Greenberg & R. N. Goldman (Eds.), *Clinical handbook of emotion-focused therapy* (pp. 61–89). American Psychological Association. https://doi.org/10.1037 /0000112-003.

Hofmann, S. G., Grossman, P., & Hinton, D. E. (2011). Loving-kindness and compassion meditation: potential for psychological interventions. *Clinical psychology review*, *31*(7), 1126–1132. https://doi.org/10.1016/j.cpr. 2011.07.003.

Hopkins J. (2001). *Cultivating compassion.* New York, NY: Broadway Books.

Horowitz, M. J. (1987). *States of Mind: Configurational analysis of individual psychology* (2nd ed.) New York: Plenum.

Liao, K.Y., Stead, G.B., & Liao, C. (2021). A Meta-Analysis of the Relation Between Self-Compassion and Self-Efficacy. *Mindfulness, 12*, 1878–1891. (2021). https://doi.org/10.1007/s12671-021-01626-4.

López, A., Sanderman, R., Ranchor, A. V., & Schroevers, M. J. (2018). Compassion for Others and Self-Compassion: Levels, Correlates, and Relationship with Psychological Well-being. *Mindfulness, 9*(1), 325–331. https://doi.org/10.1007/s12671-017-0777-z.

MacBeth, A., & Gumley, A. (2012). Exploring compassion: a meta-analysis of the association between self-compassion and psychopathology. *Clinical psychology review*, *32*(6), 545–552. https://doi.org/10.1016/j.cpr.2012. 06.003.

Neff, K. D. (2003). Self-compassion: an alternative conceptualization of a healthy attitude toward oneself. *Self and Identity, 2,* 85–102.

Neff, K. D., & Germer, C. K. (2013). A pilot study and randomized controlled trial of the mindful self-compassion program. *Journal of clinical psychology*, *69*(1), 28–44. https://doi.org/10.1002/jclp.21923.

Neff, K. D., Hseih, Y., & Dejitthirat, K. (2005). Self-compassion, achievement goals, and coping with academic failure. *Self and Identity, 4*, 263–287.

Raes, F. (2011). The effect of self-compassion on the development of depression symptoms in a non-clinical sample. *Mindfulness*, *2*, 33–36. https://doi.org/10.1007/s12671-011-0040-y.

Thimm, J.C. (2017). Relationships between early maladaptive schemas, mindfulness, self-compassion, and psychological distress. *International journal of psychology and psychological therapy, 17,* 3-17.

Wakelin, K. E., Perman, G., & Simonds, L. M. (2021). Effectiveness of self-compassion-related interventions for reducing self-criticism: A systematic review and meta-analysis. *Clinical psychology & psychotherapy*, 10.1002/cpp.2586. Advance online publication. https://doi.org/10.1002/ cpp.2586.

Wilson, A. C., Mackintosh, K., Power, K., & Chan, S. W. Y. (2019). Effectiveness of self-compassion related therapies: A systematic review and meta-analysis. *Mindfulness, 10*(6), 979–995. https://doi.org/10.1007/s12671-018-1037-6.

Young, J. E., Klosko, J. S., & Weishaar, M. E. (2003). *Schema therapy: A practitioner's guide.* New York: Guilford Press.

Zessin, U., Dickhäuser, O., & Garbade, S. (2015). The Relationship Between Self-Compassion and Well-Being: A Meta-Analysis. *Applied psychology. Health and well-being*, *7*(3), 340–364. https://doi.org/10.1111/aphw.12051.

Chapter 6

Self-Efficacy and Demographics of Greek Families with and without Members with Special Educational Needs and Disabilities during the COVID-19 Pandemic

Assimina Tsibidaki*

Department of Primary Education,
University of the Aegean, Rhodes, Greece

Abstract

Background: The COVID-19 pandemic engendered a new reality and considerable changes, with multiple psychological consequences for individuals and families. The COVID-19 pandemic and its subsequent containment are unprecedented global stressors. Research suggests that self-efficacy is one of the key resources for managing stressful events and reducing the associated risks. Self-efficacy is a general concept referring to the extent to which people believe they have the competency to cope adequately with stressful life demands or challenges.

Objectives: This study aims to explore self-efficacy and its association with demographic characteristics in Greek families of university students with or without members with special educational needs and disabilities (SEND) during the COVID-19 pandemic in Greece.

Methods: The study population consisted of 411 participants, 130 men και 281 women, of which the 194 were children (university students) in the 3rd and 4th years of their studies and the 217 were parents. The age of participants ranged from 20 to 60 years. A self-report

* Corresponding Author's Email: tsimpidaki@rhodes.aegean.gr.

In: The Importance of Self-Efficacy and Self-Compassion
Editor: James J. Carmona
ISBN: 978-1-68507-763-1

questionnaire and the Self-efficacy Scale (GSE) were used for data collection.

Results: According to the findings, participants (total sample) showed a high degree of self-efficacy during the COVID-19 pandemic and specific demographic characteristics seemed to have a significant association with self-efficacy. On one hand, there were associations between self-efficacy and a) sex, b) the family type, and d) the employment status. In particular, a higher degree of self-efficacy was shown in males, the nuclear and the extended families, the participants with no employment, and the individuals who worked from home. On the other hand, self-efficacy was not statistically significant concerning the family role (parent or child), the level of education, the existence or non-existence of one or more members with SEND in the family, and the marital status.

Conclusion: The study's main conclusion was that university students' families with or without members with SEND activated self-efficacy as a mechanism for preserving their balance during the COVID-19 pandemic and that specific individual and family demographic characteristics affect the degree of self-efficacy.

Keywords: self-efficacy, demographic characteristics, COVID-19 pandemic, families with and without members with special educational needs and disabilities (SEND), Greece

Introduction

The context of the COVID-19 pandemic is changing rapidly while the understanding of COVID-19 is constantly being developed (IASC 2020). Even though research is ongoing on the COVID-19 pandemic and on the families with members with special educational needs and disabilities (SEND), the data so far collected indicate that COVID-19 has marked a considerable change and a new reality (Toseeb et al. 2020; Tsibidaki 2021a). The COVID-19 pandemic has multiple psychological consequences for individuals and families. Therefore, the need to adapt to the new conditions by developing dynamics that enhance well-being and help dealing with the tension and worries of such a health crisis is mandatory. Self-efficacy is crucial for people's successful adaptation to the environment (Tsibidaki 2021a).

The COVID-19 pandemic and its subsequent containment are unprecedented global stressors. Research suggests that self-efficacy is one of the key resources for managing stressful events and reducing the associated risks.

Self-efficacy refers to beliefs in one's capabilities to mobilize the motivation, cognitive resources, and courses of action needed to meet given situational demands. It is a general concept referring to the extent to which people believe they have the competency to cope adequately with stressful life demands or challenges. Moreover, self-efficacy has to do with judgments about how well one can organize and execute action plans that are necessary in order to deal with possible situations that contain many ambiguous, unpredictable and often stressful elements (Bandura 1997).

Research suggests that self-efficacy is a key protective factor for families with member/s with SEND (Benzies, Trute, and Worthington 2013), in order to cope with the difficult conditions of SEND. In fact, it has been found that parents of children with SEND, although experiencing multiple challenges and difficulties, can function effectively as a system (Tsibidaki 2021a; 2021b; Tsibidaki and Tsamparli 2009). In addition, self-efficacy can empower the individual and the family with a member with SEND to handle the stressfull challenges of the COVID-19 pandemic (Tsibidaki 2021a).

This study aimed to explore self-efficacy and its association with demographic characteristics in Greek families of university students with or without members with SEND during the COVID-19 pandemic in Greece. The main research hypothesis was that participants would have a high level of anxiety and would develop high levels of self-efficacy necessary to handle the stressful event of the pandemic. In addition, we supposed that no statistically significant differences would exist on the above parameters between parents and university students. The research hypotheses were:

N1: Participants present high degree of self-efficacy.

N2: Participants' demographic characteristics present significant association with self-efficacy.

Method

Participants

The study population consisted of 411 participants, 130 (31.6%) men and 281 (68.4%) women, of which the 217 (52.8%) were parents and the 194 (47.2%)

were family members (university students) at the 3rd and 4th years of their studies and the 217 were parents. The age of participants ranged from 20 to 60 years ($M = 37.4$, $SD = 14.2$). Demographics of the participants are presented in Table 1.

Table 1. The demographics of the participants ($N = 411$)

		f	Valid %	M	SD	Min	Max
Sex	Male	130	31.6				
	Female	281	68.4				
Age		20	60	37.4	14.2	20	60
Level of Education	Tertiary education	249	60.6				
	Secondary education	63	15.3				
	PhD holder	49	11.9				
	Master's degree	45	10.9				
Marital status	Married	196	47.7				
	Single	113	27.5				
	In a relationship	86	20.9				
	Divorced	14	3.4				
	Widowed	2	0.5				
Family member	Parent	217	52.8				
	University students	194	47.2				
Type of family	Nuclear family	295	71.8				
	Single parent family	68	16.5				
	Extended family	41	10				
	Stepfamily	7	1,7				
Employment status	Full time employed	233	56.7				
	University students	100	24.3				
	Part time employed	43	10.5				
	Unemployed	26	6.3				
	Housework	9	2,2				
Work condition during lockdown	No work	208	50.6				
	Work from home	121	29.4				
	Full-time work	63	15.3				
	Part time work (some hours/days per week)	19	4.6				
Living condition during the lockdown	I live with all my family members	258	62.8				
	Alone	73	17.8				
	I live with some of my family members	36	8.8				
	I live with my partner	28	6.8				
	I live with a friend	16	3.9				

Measures

Data were collected using a Self-report Questionnaire and the General Self-Efficacy Scale (GSE). More specifically:

The Self-report Questionnaire of 13 questions was created for the study to obtain socio-demographic information such as sex, age, educational level, employment status (general and during lockdown), type of family and SEND, etc.

The General Self-Efficacy Scale (GSE) is a self-report measure of self-efficacy consisting of 10 items. The GSE is correlated to emotion, optimism and work satisfaction. Negative coefficients were found for depression, stress, health complaints, burnout and anxiety. Participants answered each item on a 4-point Likert-type scale ranging from 1 (not at all true) to 4 (exactly true). The final score is the sum of responses for each participant (Schwarzer and Jerusalem 1995). The stability of the GSE has been examined in several longitudinal studies (Schwarzer and Scholz 2000). According to Schwarzer and Jerusalem (Schwarzer and Jerusalem 1995), based on samples from 25 nations, the Cronbach's α ranged from 0.76 to 0.90, with the majority in the high 0.80. There is a Greek version of the scale. The Cronbach alpha coefficients in a Greek population were 0.77 (Glynou, Schwarzer, and Jerusalem 1994). In this study, the Cronbach alpha coefficients in total sample was 0.88 (0.89 for the parent sample and 0.87 for the university student sample).

Procedure

Data collection was carried out at the 2nd and 3rd week of the pandemic lockdown in Greece (academic year 2020-21). The briefing took place during e-Learning university lessons, where both university students and their parents completed the questionnaires using google forms.

Quantitative data analysis was based on descriptive statistics (percentages, frequencies, means, standard deviation), on criterion x2, on non-parametric test of Mann-Whitney for independent samples and on Shapiro-Wilk.

Analysis

Quantitative data analysis was based on descriptive statistics (percentages, frequencies, means, standard deviation), on criterion x2, on non-parametric test of Mann-Whitney for independent samples and on Shapiro-Wilk.

Results

Degree of Self-Efficacy

According to the findings, the participants showed a high level of self-efficacy on GSE. Moreover, there were not statistically significant differences among families with and without a member with SEND, as well as parents and university students. More specifically, for the total self-efficacy, $M = 29.50$ and $SD = 4.66$ were found and this value is higher than the average of the scale (25.00). Families with a member with a SEND showed a slightly higher average ($M = 29.75$) compared to families without a member with SEND ($M = 29.49$). Parents were found to have a slightly lower average ($M = 29.41$) than students ($M = 29.60$).

Finally, it was examined whether the variable followed the normal distribution and it was found not to follow it, because the control was not statistically significant. The results of the Shapiro-Wilk test for the self-efficacy scale were: Shapiro-Wilk: $W(61) = 0.91, p < 0.01$ for families without a member with SEND, and $W(350) = 0.92$, $p < 0.001$ for families with members with SEND. The same applied to the categories of parents and students: $W(217) = 0.94$, $p < 0.001$ for parents and $W(180) = 0.91$, $p < 0.001$ for university students.

Factors of Self-Efficacy in Relation to Demographics Characteristics

Specific demographic characteristics seemed to have a significant association with self-efficacy. More specifically, there were associations between self-efficacy and

a) sex ($p = 0.00$),

b) the family type ($p = 0.00$), and
c) the employment status ($p = 0.00$).

In particular, a higher degree of self-efficacy was shown in males, the nuclear and the extended families, the participants with no employment, and the individuals who worked from home.

Moreover, self-efficacy was not statistically significant concerning:

a) the family role (parent or child),
b) the level of education,
c) the existence or non-existence of one or more members with SEND in the family, and
d) the marital status.

Discussion

The purpose of the current study was to examine the degree of self-efficacy and its association with demographic characteristics in Greek families of university students with or without members with SEND during the COVID-19 pandemic in Greece. This study found that participants (parents and university students) showed high self-efficacy. As proposed by research on mental health and emotional impact of COVID-19, anxiety of falling sick or fear of death may amplify the sense of helplessness, hopelessness, exhaustion, burnout and nervous anticipation, negative emotions, work-life balance and personal life stressors, further compromising physical, mental and emotional wellbeing, which requires resilience (Mukhtar 2020) and self-efficacy (Tsibidaki 2021a). Moreover, this finding aligns with other research on self-efficacy noting that it functions as a protective arch aiming to manage unpredictable events and often stressful elements (Bandura 1997; Salsman et al. 2019).

Moreover, specific demographic characteristics seemed to have a significant association with self-efficacy. Literature clear patterns the influence of demographics on self-efficacy during COVID-19 (Bates et al. 2021; Tadese and Mihretie 2021; Tsibidaki 2021a). A higher degree of self-efficacy was shown in males, the nuclear and the extended families, the participants with no employment, and the individuals who worked from home. On the other hand, self-efficacy was not statistically significant concerning the family role (parent or child), the level of education, the existence or non-existence of one or more members with SEND in the family, and the marital status.

Limitations of the Study

The results of the present study should be cautiously treated since they are based on a specific group derived from the Greek population. Another limitation is that this study was a survey-based research, and the results came solely from questionnaires. A mixed method combining both quantitative (e.g., questionnaires) and qualitative data (e.g., semi-structured interviews) could give more profound evidence on self-efficacy in families of university students belonging to families with and without SEND.

Conclusion

Parents and university students demonstrate higher meaning in life (presence), general self-efficacy and resilience (than the scale average).

The general conclusion of this study is that university students' families with one or more members with SEND activated self-efficacy as a mechanism for preserving their balance and that specific individual and family demographic characteristics affect the degree of self-efficacy.

References

Bandura, Albert. 1997. *Self-Efficacy: The Exercise of Control*. Self-Efficacy: The Exercise of Control. New York, NY, US: W H Freeman/Times Books/ Henry Holt & Co.

Bates, Carolyn R., Laura M. Nicholson, Elizabeth M. Rea, Hannah A. Hagy, and Amy M. Bohnert. 2021. "Life Interrupted: Family Routines Buffer Stress during the COVID-19 Pandemic." *Journal of Child and Family Studies* 30 (11): 2641–51. https://doi.org/10. 1007/s10826-021-02063-6.

Benzies, Karen M., Barry Trute, and Catherine Worthington. 2013. "Maternal Self-Efficacy and Family Adjustment in Households with Children with Serious Disability." *Journal of Family Studies* 19 (1): 35–43. https://doi.org/10.5172/jfs.2013.19.1.35.

Glynou, Ekaterini, Ralf Schwarzer, and Matthias Jerusalem. 1994. "*Greek Adaptation of the General Self-Efficacy Scale*." 1994. http://userpage.fu-berlin.de/~health/greek.htm.

IASC, Inter-Agency Standing Committee. 2020. "*Interim Guidance on Scaling-up COVID-19 Outbreak in Readiness and Response Operations in Camps and Camp-like Settings (Jointly Developed by IFRC, IOM, UNHCR and WHO) | IASC*." March 17, 2020. https:// interagencystandingcommittee.org/other/interim-guidance-scaling-covid-19-outbreak-readiness-and-response-operations-camps-and-camp.

Mukhtar, Sonia. 2020. "Mental Health and Emotional Impact of COVID-19: Applying Health Belief Model for Medical Staff to General Public of Pakistan." *Brain, Behavior, and Immunity* 87 (July): 28–29. https://doi.org/10.1016/j.bbi.2020.04.012.

Salsman, John M., Benjamin D. Schalet, Thomas V. Merluzzi, Crystal L. Park, Elizabeth A. Hahn, Mallory A. Snyder, and David Cella. 2019. "Calibration and Initial Validation of a General Self-Efficacy Item Bank and Short Form for the NIH PROMIS®." *Quality of Life Research* 28 (9): 2513–23. https://doi.org/10.1007/s11136-019-02198-6.

Schwarzer, Ralf, and Matthias Jerusalem. 1995. "Generalized Self-Efficacy Scale." In *Measures in Health Psychology: A User's Portfolio. Causal and Control Beliefs*, Measures in health psychology: A user's portfolio. Causal and control beliefs:35–37. Windsor, UK: NFER-NELSON.

Schwarzer, Ralf, and Urte Scholz. 2000. "Cross-Cultural Assessment of Coping Resources: The General Perceived Self-Efficacy Scale." Presented at the *First Asian Congress of Health Psychology: Health Psychology and Culture, Tokyo, Japan*. http://userpage.fu-berlin.de/gesund/skalen/Language_Selection/Turkish/General_Perceived_Self-Efficac/hauptteil_general_perceived_self-efficac.htm.

Tadese, Mesfin, and Abebe Mihretie. 2021. "Attitude, Preparedness, and Perceived Self-Efficacy in Controlling COVID-19 Pandemics and Associated Factors among University Students during School Reopening." *PLOS ONE* 16 (9): e0255121. https://doi.org/10. 1371/journal.pone.0255121.

Toseeb, Umar, Dr Kathryn Asbury, Aimee Code, Laura Fox, and Emre Deniz. 2020. "*Supporting Families with Children with Special Educational Needs and Disabilities during COVID-19*," April. https://doi.org/10.31234/osf.io/tm69k.

Tsibidaki, Assimina. 2021a. "Anxiety, Meaning in Life, Self-Efficacy and Resilience in Families with One or More Members with Special Educational Needs and Disability during COVID-19 Pandemic in Greece." *Research in Developmental Disabilities* 109 (February): 103830. https://doi.org/10.1016/j.ridd.2020.103830.

———. 2021b. "Children with Cerebral Palsy: Family and Parent Demographic Characteristics and Family Strengths in Greece and Italy." *Journal of Health Psychology* 26 (12): 2071–83. https:// doi.org/10.1177/1359105319900276.

Tsibidaki, Assimina, and Anastasia Tsamparli. 2009. "Adaptability and Cohesion of Greek Families: Raising a Child with a Severe Disability on the Island of Rhodes." *Journal of Family Studies* 15 (3): 245–59. https://doi.org/10.5172/jfs.15.3.245.

Index

U